I0789861

1000 Days in Gaza

Cover design: KBR

Image by Susan Ruggles from Milwaukee, USA - 0078, CC BY 2.0, https://commons.wikimedia.org/w/index.php?curid=105704938

ISBN 978-1-944608-76-7

Library of Congress Control Number: 2026938483

Published by KBR

KBR Digital LLC

www.kbrdigital.com

1 | 864 | 373.4528

Greenville, South Carolina

April 2026

Printed in the United States

A document that was written because it had to exist.

For Alan, as always. And for my two wonderful sons, who allowed me the pleasures of motherhood later in life.

For my parents, who made my life worthwhile as a Sabra by teaching me Jewish values and the love of Israel.

Contents

Part One

2023

Mice and... Men?

October 8

The best-laid plans of mice and men gang aft agley. —
Robert Burns (1759-1796)

Last Monday, at 3 a.m., a popular New York "community organizer" was returning from a wedding when, suddenly and without warning, a stranger stabbed him in front of his girlfriend.

The organizer, unfortunately, did not survive.

The video — which can be seen online — leaves some room for doubt: Did the girlfriend know the killer?

In the days that followed, the victim's many "friends," including his girlfriend, refused to condemn the murderer. Believe it or not, they chose loyalty to "community ideals" over justice, even going so far as to say the victim himself would have "preferred" to defend the murderer rather than mourn the loss of his own life.

Give me a break.

They even created a GoFundMe campaign to raise funds — not for funeral expenses or to support the family, but so they could "properly mourn the loss of their friend."

Very good friends!

This is just another sign of the absurd times we're living in, where moral and cultural rules have been inverted in an attempt to irrevocably subvert our understanding of the world. We're so immersed in constant lies that the media — followed by the American government — has lost all sense of judgment and no longer even tries to disguise the gaslighting.

Also this week, I read an article in *The New York Times* daily newsletter explaining how Republicans were creating major hurdles around the renewal of the government budget, putting the lives and survival of millions of people at risk. Only in the last line did the author inform the reader that, in fact, Republicans had already voted for the renewal the previous week.

In yet another newsletter that same week, the same *New York Times* tried to blame Republicans for all the country's problems — a dominant trend in the media — including an interview with Hillary Clinton in which she states that Republicans need to be subjected to a "forced deprogramming." I swear to God. Yet, as everyone knows, the country has been governed by the Democrats for almost three years.

Problems are exploding from all sides: the gender cult, defunding the police, inflation, and rampant drug addiction, not to mention the unspeakable numbers of illegal immigrants, but the "do-gooders" don't seem willing to admit their mistakes. Quite the contrary: The blame lies entirely with the Republicans and — get ready for this — with Donald Trump, a kind of eternal punching bag they are trying to eliminate in every possible way, except (for now) by assassination. That is an inexcusable premise I didn't raise, God forbid; it was Tucker Carlson, the former anchor and current podcaster on X, who did it.

Life has become so absurd that, in *The Middle Way*, I made a point of linking every outrageous statement, no matter how small, so you don't think I'm exaggerating.

The most pathetic proof was the superhuman effort undertaken by various sectors of the government this week — President Biden and Homeland Security Secretary Alejandro Mayorkas included — to reinforce their position against building a wall on the Mexican border, even while stating, in no uncertain terms, that the government was resuming construction.

This is doublethink to the nth degree! Not even George Orwell could have dared so much! They say life imitates art, but life is now intensifying art in the worst sense, because nothing good can come from these incompetent madmen.

The problem with the wall is that Donald Trump — the renegade, the despicable, the repeatedly judged and eternally condemned Donald Trump — made the wall his biggest electoral promise in 2016, (I should note that I don't even wish to see him back in the White House, although the alternatives are becoming more limited by the day) fulfilled only in part due to Democrat resistance.

During the "Trump Years," immigration was under control, thanks to the wall, clever agreements with Mexico, and efficient policing. But when Biden took office with his cohort of globalists, the first thing he did was cancel the construction. He went even further: All the construction material, mostly steel, was summarily auctioned off at 10 cents on the dollar — practically thrown into the trash of history.

With the propaganda favoring a completely open border, we saw a flood — an invasion — not only of illegal immigrants, but of South American gang members, drug traffickers, child exploiters, and wanted terrorists from the Middle East. It was chaos, totally predictable and largely ignored, until the Governor of Texas had the brilliant idea of putting immigrants on buses to "sanctuary" cities like New York, Chicago, and even Martha's Vineyard, the sacrosanct resort of the wealthy, including former President Obama.

As a result, the left-leaning patriots, who considered themselves safe from the invasion, were unable to deal with the situation. It was astonishing to see New Yorkers screaming hysterically against the influx of immigrants. Finally, this week, Mayor Eric Adams — who is black and a Democrat — was forced to declare that he would no longer condone the... well, in-va-sion.

The federal government could no longer pretend nothing was happening and decided to declare it was being "forced" to obey a congressional directive to resume construction. I won't even bother reminding you that this directive was approved more than four years ago!

This is already getting too long, but I must add to this list of failures a new war between Israelis and Palestinians, which erupted this Saturday morning. Everyone on TV is talking about it, and, fortunately, the majority are in favor of Israel.

As you know, in recent months Israel has been infected by the virus of meaninglessness, with protests and reservists threatening to abandon military service in response to policies proposed by Netanyahu — which, incidentally, were very poorly explained by the leftist media.

The highly competent Israeli secret service — the legendary Mossad — must have been distracted by the "woke" approach forced upon them. That is the only explanation. The end result was that, just as in the Yom Kippur War exactly 50 years ago, the country was caught by surprise.

My husband Alan always told me that the only way to end this moral and cultural bankruptcy would be a war, but I honestly never expected it to take place in my beloved and mistreated homeland.

May God protect us. At least in Israel, Alan's recipe seems to be working: The country is now united, and the reservists are showing up in droves to defend it.

Mourning and Solidarity

October 11

Amidst the grief that has descended upon our home and, I believe, upon all Jewish homes throughout the world, rare moments of hope offer consolation coming from where it's least expected.

Yesterday, I spent the entire day hearing repeatedly, hundreds of times, that the bodies of 200 adults and 40 babies, some decapitated, had been found in Kfar Azza.

Decapitated babies! I couldn't take it anymore. I had about ten minutes of a genuine nervous breakdown, and Alan was frightened. I was forced to request extensions for several deadlines.

This story about decapitated babies deeply affected me. I believe there were so many because, in general, babies in kibbutzim sleep together under supervision, separated from their parents (though I'm not sure if that's still the case). I myself slept in one of those dormitories during my first year of life, in the kibbutz Afikim.

There are a lot of disgusting people here in the US, including the student elite at Harvard University, who are approving of

what Hamas did and blaming Israel for the violence we were subjected to.

So, it was with enormous surprise that I watched a meeting
between Joe Biden and leaders of the Jewish community, organized by the husband of Vice President Kamala Harris — who is
Jewish (a fact we rarely remember). You know how much I detest
Biden and how I criticize him day and night; yes, I blame him for
the misery leftists and "progressives" are causing us. But the
president (it's the first time I have proudly associated the title
with the man) was impeccable: no teleprompter, no stuttering,
no memory lapses, and with his heart in the right place.

Farewell to Illusions

October 14

> *...a time to love and a time to hate; a time to fight and a
> time to live in peace.* — Ecclesiastes 3:8

Today I got rid of my beautiful red keffiyeh, which I had preserved carefully and lovingly for 53 years. My fellow kibbutz
members from the past who read me here on *The Middle Way*
will surely remember my pride when wearing it wrapped around
my neck.

The year was 1970, and we were spending a year in Israel,
alternating different kibbutzim, and what we loved more than
anything was going for walks in Jerusalem, specifically in the Arab
market.

We loved everything Arabic: the food, the clothes, the ven-
dors in the souk, with whom we had fun being forced to haggle
over every penny, not to mention the profanities. (There are no

profanities in Hebrew, an ancient sacred biblical language, so we used Arabic ones, *con mucho gusto*.)

I had a special fondness for a black Arabic dress embroidered with orange and yellow that I lost over time, but which I still remember in minute detail. I also had another dress, orange this time — my favorite color — with the chest entirely embroidered. Both were very beautiful, and I always wore them with pride.

It turns out that I lost the dresses, but not the keffiyeh. It accompanied me through my many moves — life changes, changes of husband, changes of location: from Belo Horizonte to Rio; from Rio to Brasília; from Brasília to Pirenópolis; from Pirenópolis back to Rio; from Rio to St. Augustine (in Florida, US); from St. Augustine back to Rio; from Rio to Itaipava; and, finally, from Itaipava to Greenville. Once here, the red keffiyeh was carefully folded and kept in the small apartment where we lived while building our house in the mountains, and later in the closet of our beautiful home.

I kept it with tender loving care all this time, practically my whole adult life... until today. Last Saturday, I started looking at the keffiyeh with different eyes and thinking about getting rid of it. Finally, today, when Alan and I were gathering some clothes and shoes to donate to charity, I decided that the time had come to "get rid of this dead weight in my life," as the lyric Brazilian songwriter Chico Buarque put it poetically when I was young.

It was a difficult week. Every scene on TV depicting young Americans wrapped in keffiyehs, waving Palestinian flags and shouting slogans against Israel and the Jews made my stomach churn. So today, finally, was my decision day.

At first, I thought about adding the keffiyeh, which despite being so old still looked brand new, to the donation bag, but then I thought it over. If I did that, very soon another person, as deluded as I once was with ideals of peace and equality throughout the world, would be wearing it with "pride" while, God forbid, demonstrating in favor of the Palestinian "cause."

But bringing along my ex-beloved keffiyeh? No chance.

So, I took the beautiful red keffiyeh, carefully preserved for almost 54 years — a sweet reminder of the idealistic young woman I once was — out of the donation bag and threw it in the trash.

Then I hesitated. I took it out of the trash, soaked it in bleach, put it back in the middle of the kitchen garbage, and immediately went outside in the rain and threw it in the large, black trash can — the one constantly violated by the hungry bears that live in our forest — and mixed it well with the rotten and smelly food scraps.

Since today is Saturday, the bin is full to the top with the week's trash. Last night, despite our multiple efforts to keep the bears away, one of them showed up, knocked the very heavy trash can over, managed to open all the security latches (besides being huge and strong, they are intelligent animals) and tore to pieces the several supermarket bags we use for trash, scattering the debris all over the garden.

Now here I am, praying that the bear comes back tonight and tears my once-beautiful red keffiyeh to shreds, leaving not a single trace of it.

Amen.

They Came with Everything, and Then Some

October 15

An impressive video circulating on the internet shows sophisticated weapons captured from Hamas terrorists, including devices that cause the temperature of a room to rise suddenly

and rapidly through spontaneous combustion, essentially burning the occupants alive with no possibility of escape.

This was one of Hamas's favorite "tactics" last week: Firing
rockets to frighten the kibbutz residents, forcing them to take
shelter in the "panic rooms" (which are mandatory in all kibbutz
houses) and then burning them alive.

The video appears to be a live feed (I watched it a few minutes ago on YouTube). Therefore, you need to go back to the beginning to see the IDF spokesperson displaying the seized
weapons.

The Calm After the Storm
(But When? And at What Price?)

October 16

Many contend that while the cannons are smoking, it's not
exactly the best time to think about the future or envision a way
out of this bottomless pit. Now, it is true that focusing on loss,
tragedy, graphic images and the flow of blood 24 hours a day
would drive anyone crazy.

This was almost happening to me (going crazy). So, because I
have daily obligations and survival needs that can't be ignored, I
decided to turn off the TV for a few hours. Next, I tried to seek
out the voices I most admire, away from the deafening noise of
the "news business."

That was how I came across a brilliant interview by Lex Fridman with Jared Kushner.

I know quite a bit about the history of Israel, but not so much
about the present day — that is, the present day before October
7. The interview is long, but the first 60 minutes shed light on the
current situation from the perspective of one of the most

creative and audacious negotiators of our time: Jared Kushner, Donald Trump's favorite son-in-law.

Right off the bat, we understand why the left is so keen to portray Jared as a dishonest capitalist whose only interest in the Middle East negotiations during the Trump administration — when important advances were made that, as Jared points out, were methodically destroyed by the current administration — was to make a few billion dollars in real estate ventures.

I wonder if these sycophants are now seething with regret at the widespread mess that resulted from their thoughtless actions.

Yes, Jared worked toward establishing business partnerships between traditional enemies, instead of focusing on politics, a strategy that previously failed to achieve any substance in the region. But don't let yourselves be fooled: Jared didn't do this out of greed or a desire to amass power. Simply put, his capitalist focus was precisely the stroke of genius that made the Abraham Accords possible.

Despite the sadness of the past few days, Jared doesn't seem to have given up. Although his advice is to let things be still while "what needs to happen happens," the skilled negotiator does see a path to the future, and we really want to believe in that.

I don't know if you watched it, but about two weeks ago, MBS — the Crown Prince of Saudi Arabia and *de facto* king of the Muslim giant (since his father, the *de jure* king, is more dead than alive) made it very clear in a series of interviews with Fox News, in perfect English, that an agreement with Israel was very close.

It is widely believed that this possibility was the trigger for Iran to launch a proxy attack, as Jared explains.

Check it out. It's worth every minute of your time.

Yossi Landau: A Firsthand Account

October 17

The days keep going and we think we've heard everything, but the truth is the stories are only just beginning.

Today I broke down in tears again listening to an interview with Yossi Landau, the former head of a team of experienced rescue workers who worked in the rubble after 9/11.

Yes, both here and in Israel, the October 7 attack has been compared to 9/11, and I was "lucky" enough to have witnessed both events.

I remember it as if it was yesterday, watching the first World Trade Center building collapse from the locker room of a gym in Rio de Janeiro, getting home in time to urge my mother to "turn on the TV because something was happening," and watching the second building fall live.

I dare say that October 7 was far worse than September 11. On 9/11, 3,000 people died when the buildings they were in were hit by planes and collapsed. For a few minutes, they knew how it was going to end, and then it did.

But on October 7, people took much longer to die. They were treated personally, as "individual cases," and tortured, raped, burned, and had body parts severed before being finally terminated by terrorists who are worse than Hitler's henchmen — and this is the very first time I have said something like this, breaking a personal oath to "never compare anything or anyone to Hitler and Nazism," because, frankly, I didn't believe this could happen again.

Incidentally, we usually see Nazi atrocities only in movies, but this time, we witnessed them happening in real time, live, on TV, on our cell phones, not as a dismissible historical account — as

Holocaust deniers like to do. All of it was concentrated in just one day and with a huge body count.

In another interview with Fox ten minutes ago, Yossi said he had already collected 700 bodies, most heavily mutilated and many burned alive.

Am Israel Chai

October 18

At the end of his speech, Biden said he would repeat the classic Jewish saying — Am Israel Chai — in English because "he wasn't good with languages."

Biden might not be good at many things — at most things, we should say — but for now, I'm taking a break from my criticism.

Over a year ago, during the President's speech in Europe, someone said that Biden was "speaking from the heart," and I said: "No, 'he is speaking from the teleprompter.'" But today, I take back what I said.

This morning (afternoon local time), in Israel, Biden indeed spoke from the heart.

No matter what kind of negotiations are unfolding behind the scenes: Secretary of State Antony Blinken has been traveling back and forth in the region for over seven days, and Biden, let's face it, showed a lot of guts by getting directly involved in this extremely dangerous situation.

All of this proves, beyond a shadow of a doubt, that, despite detractors to the contrary, the United States indeed "stands with Israel."

The most recent source of suffering stems from yesterday's alleged explosion at a Gaza hospital, which killed over 500 people. Predictably, Hamas and the antisemitic mob didn't hesitate for a second to accuse Israel.

However:

1. Israel does not bomb hospitals full of sick civilians.

2. Israel published a recorded conversation in which Hamas commanders affirm that the rocket came from an Islamic terrorist organization.

Israel has confirmed that the hospital explosion showed no signs of being an air strike (which would have originated from Is-rael). On the contrary, it was caused by a land-based rocket.

I'm obviously well aware that, in the media, whoever shouts the loudest succeeds in imposing their opinion... which, generally speaking, is usually the opposite of the truth.

Meanwhile, we are left with the symbolism of Biden's presence and the ancient words: "Am Israel Chai" (The people of Israel live on.)

If I'm Jewish, Am I Not Black?

October 19

I apologize, but I couldn't resist the parody of the famous line from Shylock's monologue in *The Merchant of Venice*: "If you hurt us, do we not bleed?"

Furthermore, I deliberately wanted to allude to Black Lives Matter, which is one of the topics of the video I'm recommending today — in which you can see a Black Jewish woman, a former Miss Israel, speaking out on Fox's prime-time news last night against this state of affairs where most "peace-loving" protesters around the world are actually celebrating terrorism and violence.

I'll let Yityish Aynaw speak for herself. No matter how much I write, my forcefulness will never reach her level.

One of the most prominent subjects discussed yesterday was the denial of the terrible "bombing" of the Palestinian hospital that "killed" 500 people, mostly children. The news spread like wildfire the second after the explosion, published by Hamas without any effort to verify it.

The entire media swallowed it.

However, after extensive research and technical corroboration, the conclusion was not only that Israel did not bomb the hospital, but, worse still, that there was no bombing whatsoever. As the story goes, no one really knows how many people died when a rocket fired by a terrorist organization malfunctioned and fell into a parking lot behind the hospital, creating a small crater and a lot of smoke.

These proven facts, of course, did not prevent an American congresswoman from leading a tearful demonstration in Washington because "Israelis were killing children," most likely well aware that all this was a lie because the debunking had already been published.

In the image, compiled by Bari Weiss, we can see how *The New York Times* kept changing its headlines as the truth unfolded.

There Is No Country Called Palestine

October 21

At first glance, you might think that the title of my note is racist, Islamophobic, or whatever other cliché you can think of.

It is not.

It is simply a statement of fact.

There is no country called "Palestine," despite my native Brazil being one among several UN member states that recognize one. There is, however, a proposed country with that name and an official Palestinian Authority that advocates for the creation of such a country, whose leader is Mahmoud Abbas, and which is headquartered in the West Bank.

Obviously, the media and activists in the last 15 days have turned the existence of Palestine into an official fact — as official as the bombing of the hospital in Gaza by Israeli forces that never happened.

The curious thing is that, at the beginning of the 20th century, and for centuries before that, there was indeed a territory known as Palestine. My grandfather, for example, emigrated to Brazil in 1910, and his passport stated that he came from Palestine.

Now, what never existed was a country called Palestine that *belonged to the Arabs.*

My grandfather's country of origin was a direct heir to biblical Canaan, which, according to the Bible, was promised by God to the "people of the book"— that is, the Jews — more than 5,000 years ago. But the political reality of the 20th and 21st centuries has never been very inclined to grant the "God-promised" country to its rightful owners. The people who live there were forced to take it by force, and to this day the situation remains the same.

It is curious to see in the picture above the term "climate justice" mixed up with "freedom for Palestine" — two unproven claims for nonexistent things. Yesterday's edition of Michael Shellenberger's *Public* explains that the stuffed toy octopus seen above the right shoulder of "vigilante" Greta Thunberg is "a symbol frequently used by anti-Jewish propaganda since it was first used in a Nazi-era cartoon."

No wonder. All the banners raised by the "woke crowd" in demonstrations are based on nonexistent premises that contradict reality, as I have always been keen to point out in my essays. "Freedom for Palestinians" is just another example.

The only thing standing between the Palestinians and freedom is their own government — a terrorist group called Hamas. Everything else you're hearing is just propaganda.

In his column yesterday, Shellenberger expressed hope that the events of October 7 are signaling the end of wokeism.

But at what price?

And just so it doesn't seem like everything we talked about today is purely pessimistic, let's take a minute to celebrate the release of two Hamas hostages yesterday — a mother and daughter.

According to sources, there are still *only* 208 to go, including children, disabled people, and even infants, but the self-appointed "guardians of humanity" seem to have forgotten this irrelevant fact in their demands for an immediate "ceasefire."[1]

So far, we have not received an account of the horrors that the two American women witnessed and were subjected to. I'm pretty sure they weren't treated with kid gloves, or, as Americans usually say, with "tender loving care."

Have a nice weekend.

Guiltless Antisemitism

October 22

The friendly-looking woman in the news today is the president of a synagogue in Detroit, USA.

Or should I say former president? Samantha Woll, president of the board of the Isaac Agree Downtown Synagogue in Detroit, was fatally stabbed early Saturday morning. The police urged

---

[1] A correction: The IDF informs that there are 210, not 208, hostages retained by Hamas, 30 of them children. Each person counts.

calm and refused to associate the murder with the situation in the Middle East.

Look, I've never subscribed to the idea that antisemitism is common, that it's everywhere, and that we should protect ourselves against it. As a child in Brazil, I attended a Christian school where I had to pray the Hail Mary before classes. I attended high school at the Minas Gerais State College, a public school, and studied architecture at Saint Úrsula University in Rio. I don't know exactly who Saint Ursula was, but even today I'm able to recite the Hail Mary prayer in Latin.

I have no recollection of experiencing antisemitism in my youth, and living as a minority in a Catholic country never bothered me. However, this was probably associated with the existence of the State of Israel, a "lifelong guarantee" that Jews are now protected from all evil after the horrors of Nazism — poignantly portrayed in a German film I watched yesterday on Amazon Prime, *Labyrinth of Lies*, about the "Frankfurt Trials" I had never heard of.

This morning, while being "massacred" (once again!) in the comments section of *The Times* of London for trying to explain the difference between the Palestinian and the Israeli victims in the Gaza war, I found myself wondering what would have happened if people in Europe in 1940 had been anything like those who today lament and equate the Palestinian victims in the bombing of a church in Gaza to the victims of the October 7 attack. And not only that: They loudly protest in public in favor of Hamas with antisemitic[2] slogans.

------

[2] We have been debating for a while whether we should spell the term as "anti-Semitism," "anti-Semitic," or the more modern forms, "antisemitic," "antisemitism." In an extensive article published by The Times of Israel in 2018, the non-hyphenated form seems to be gaining ground, so, in this book, we decided to adopt it.

Don't get me wrong. I feel sorry for the Palestinian civilian victims and would obviously prefer that everyone lived in peace in the region. But can anyone imagine protests in the streets all over the world (outside of Germany and Austria, of course) in favor of Hitler? In favor of the Japanese after Pearl Harbor? Can anyone out there imagine crowds in the streets criticizing the Normandy invasion and lamenting the destruction of Dresden?

I don't think so.

If that were ultimately the case, these well-meaning Englishmen probably wouldn't be here to express their guiltless anti-semitism in the comments section of their favorite newspaper. They would probably, let's face it, be forced to speak German and greet people on the street with a raised arm.

Not Even Al Jazeera Can Handle It

October 24

One incorrect news report from *The New York Times* was enough to set the masses in an uproar last weekend, shouting in the streets and demanding that "all Jews be killed in the gas chamber."

Due to the irresponsible attitude of "the most important newspaper in the world" — as Bari Weiss reports in her column in *The Free Press* today — a synagogue was completely destroyed by fire in Tunisia.

However, despite the lightweight denial mentioned by Bari, it seems that *The New York Times* has learned nothing. In today's newsletter, there it was again: a news bulletin sent by the Hamas "Ministry of Health" stating that more than 5,000 people had already died due to Israeli bombings.

Meanwhile, in the real world, two women hostages — one 79 years old and the other 85 — were released yesterday by Hamas "for humanitarian reasons." Their husbands, who are even older, remain in captivity. Notably, one of them is a peace activist whose daily work involved entering Gaza and bringing sick people from there to hospitals in Israel.

As Alan always says, "no good deed goes unpunished."

While major Western news outlets continue to stumble in their attempt to balance on the tightrope of news interpretation — oscillating between rightfully accusing Israel *comme il faut* and exonerating the terrorists — *Al Jazeera*, surprisingly, seems to be unable to tolerate the cruelty of these animals. You can check their interview with one of the hostages, Yocheved Lifshitz, 85, in which the official TV station of the Arab world seems to show some sympathy for the victim.

On "our side," in a statement yesterday, Fox correspondent Trey Yingst lost his composure while reporting live on the horrors documented and proven by Israel, which felt compelled to present this evidence to the international press in light of the mountain of lies in favor of Hamas that were being spread — including the misinformation affirming that no decapitated babies ever existed. In other words, that they were nothing but "Zionist propaganda."

According to Trey's account, a captured terrorist told his interrogators that "the commanders told us to step on civilians' heads, decapitate them, do whatever we felt like." The interrogator then asked him to compare himself to ISIS, and he agreed, saying the following: "We burn, we slaughter, we decapitate people."

Trey said in his report that "he would need to censor the brutality expressed by the captured terrorist while the man admitted to having done things that human beings don't do."

Disunited Nations
Extra Edition

October 24

It's been a long time since we found out that a good part of the evil that plagues this world — based on nonsensical premises of "equity," "climate threats," "thousands of genders," and all other false narratives of modernity — originates from the United Nations and its billions of committees that consume the billions of dollars they receive in contributions, mostly from the United States. But I honestly never expected to hear the Secretary-General of that failed institution, the Portuguese António Guterres, JUSTIFY the terrorist attacks of October 7.

How embarrassing!

Does he know what he's talking about? Did he truly UNDERSTAND his statement, written in English by somebody else, as is customary?

The statement immediately triggered a diplomatic incident with Israel, whose ambassador to the UN canceled the meeting scheduled with the so-called "secretary-general."

Does this mean the United Nations endorses the slogans being shouted everywhere asking to send the Jews to gas chambers? Do they endorse the decapitated bodies? The chants for the elimination of the State of Israel? Celebrating the "intifada"?

They will soon feel the crushing weight of the United States' veto power. I surely hope they also lose their beautiful rental building where they keep spouting nonsense in the center of New York City.

***

Unbelievable. After posting this essay, I kept researching and came across this statement from the United Nations condemning the "brutal bombing of the hospital in Gaza," which, as we all know too well, never happened. The same statement demands that countries "reverse the dangers that threaten people with albinism."

In case someone comes to their senses and decides to delete this "official" pile of lies, I'm posting a screenshot here to prove it for posterity.

"Why, (Ye'll Say) 'Tis Sure Thou Hast Lost Thy Senses!"[3]

October 26

Another unbelievable event: Yesterday, 10 days after that bomb failed to fall on the Gaza hospital and kill 500 people, *The New York Times* sent an email to their humongous contact list — including non-subscribers, or I wouldn't have received it — in which they explain how they hired an entire team and acquired numerous videos from various sources, with the sole purpose of proving that Israel — and also American, British and other intelligence sources — are lying and that, in fact, the bombing did occur.

I don't recommend that you read the article; it's extremely confusing, and somewhere in the middle the text keeps affirming that there was no bombing, at least not at that hospital.

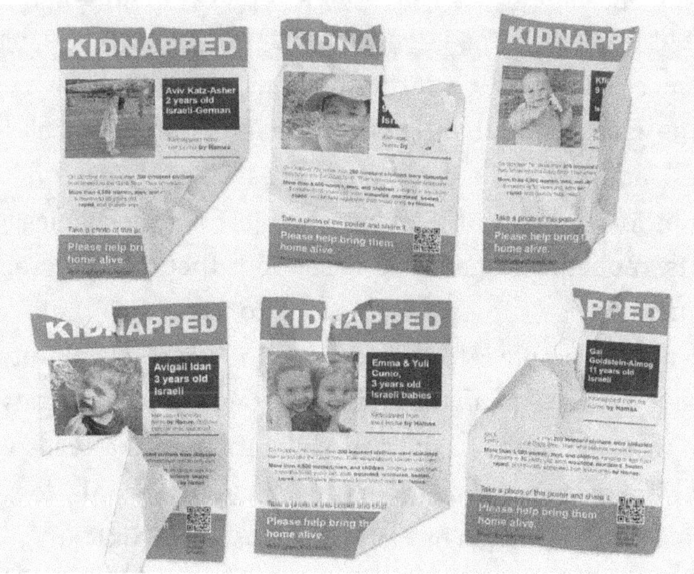

---

[3] The title of this essay is a quote by the Brazilian poet Olavo Bilac, but with an implicit meaning far less sweet than that of the beautiful sonnet.

Confusion and information overload are not innocent tactics, but a preferred strategy for those who thrive in manipulating public opinion.

As I clarified above, the UN also maintains a statement on its website condemning the bombing, along with the same old rehearsed rhetoric that includes climate change and transgender issues — pressing issues, which, by the way, were also highlighted in the pathetic speeches uttered by Biden and the Australian Prime Minister at their meeting yesterday in the White House.

The world is going to smithereens and the "leaders of the free world" keep insisting on "climate, climate, climate."

And why am I insisting as well?

While researching the Brazilian newspaper *Folha de S. Paulo*, I realized that, in Brazil, the issue of this war doesn't even exist, so I apologize for insisting on a subject that is vitally important to me, but probably of no importance to you, fellow Brazilians.

The crucial question at this moment is how this war is exposing the fallacies and craziness of these people who call themselves "activists." It is becoming increasingly obvious that they are not in the habit of thinking; they just act mechanically, like robots, repeating slogans and falsehoods that make no sense to anyone who dedicates a mere second to using their brain.

A good example is today's story in *The Free Press* about these activists who are out in the streets of major American cities tearing down photos of kidnapped children from the walls where they were pasted, calling them (the children, I mean) "dogs" and praying that they rot in hell in videos posted on TikTok.

Children! Babies! For 20 days in the hands of cruel and brainless terrorists!

May God protect them (the children, of course).
Nothing else needs to be said.

"Unanimity" and the War of Words
Or... A War for Which I Have No Words

October 27

I wasn't exactly watching; I was just listening when the Fox announcer, without a shadow of a doubt, asserted that the UN had "unanimously adopted a resolution demanding that Israel enter into a 'humanitarian' truce with Hamas."

The absurdity peaked a minute later, when I watched the US ambassador to the UN say that the resolution was a disgrace for not even mentioning the violence of the October 7 terrorist attack.

It is glaringly obvious to me that the term "unanimity" was terribly misused by the reporter, but the reality isn't much better: Only 14 countries (out of the 193 that make up the General Assembly, which hardly deserves its capital letters) voted against it — among them the United States.

Please don't ask me how my native Brazil voted. My former homeland is an international shame for sure, always siding against what could be considered a just opinion.

Canada tried hard to salvage humanity's honor from this embarrassment by proposing an amendment that emphasized the "deliberate cruelty" regarding the October 7 attacks. It was defeated. What disappointed me, however, was the ultimate lack of courage on Canada's part: When the time came to vote on the final resolution, instead of voting against it, they preferred to abstain.

Canada's reputation couldn't go any lower here at home, but I'll give them the benefit of the doubt, attributing this cowardly vote to the "rules of diplomacy," which I prefer to ignore. Perhaps, after having proposed an amendment — which, in the current absurd circumstances, can be considered an act of enormous courage — and having been defeated, the diplomatic norm is to abstain. Who knows.

At any rate, here we are, with yet another useless UN resolution that isn't worth the ink used to write it, because it so happens that General Assembly resolutions have no legal value, and are nothing but empty talk.

So tonight, as I write, stumbling over my words from so much outrage, Israel has finally launched its ground operation to complete the elimination of Hamas without leaving a trace.

The argument being made around the world tonight is that, while Hamas has killed 1,500 people with extreme cruelty and in direct confrontation, and is still holding 224 hostages (yes, despite the four hostages being released, the number continues to rise, instead of falling), Israel has already killed more than 7,000 Palestinians (numbers deemed "indisputable" by Hamas's supposed "Ministry of Health"). These people seem incapable of distinguishing between victims of torture and deliberate murder and the unintended victims of a war.

A war that, incidentally, Israel did not provoke, nor want. But don't let yourselves be fooled, my friends: Tonight, I am praying for the total and definitive victory of Israel.

Those who are bothered by this should leave the premises immediately.

Shabbat Shalom!

Queers for Palestine

October 28

> *Forgive them, Lord, for they know not what they do. —*
> *Luke 23:34*

Despite all the pain of the last 22 days, we have to admit that certain moments of this war-torn saga are sheer comedy.

As I write, the streets of London are filled with trendy protesters chanting against Israel and in favor of Palestinians.

The historical ignorance of these deluded youngsters is astounding.

It is clear to anyone with even less than a cubic inch of gray matter within their battered skulls that they haven't the slightest idea of what they're defending, and in today's note I'm not referring to the cruel and indisputable hand-to-hand murder of over 1,500 innocent civilians — including children and babies — many decapitated, others with fingers and toes severed and other details that seem more like something out of a series of blood-soaked movies that, here in the US, we like to watch in the Halloween season, such as the classic *The Texas Chainsaw Massacre*.

The details of the severed hands and feet, as well as the brutally gouged-out eyes, which I hadn't even heard of until yesterday, are reminiscent of Sharia Law, which the modern types of this world also like to celebrate, not to mention the stupid women who voluntarily cover themselves from head to toe with "charming" hijabs at demonstrations, an offense to the poor victims of Islamic fundamentalism who are *forced* to wear the garment along with other drastic restrictions on their freedom.

Ironically, other signs at the "Queers for Palestine" marches — of course, in this context, the term "queer" has possibly lost any other meaning except the privileged class of special humans protected and blessed by God in every corner of this Earth — show the slogan "Abortionists for Palestine," ignoring the fact that "reproductive rights" are strictly prohibited in Gaza and other places governed by Islamic fundamentalists, along with all other women's rights, with or without quotation marks.

In short: There are no women's rights in Islamic countries. Period. Nor are there LGBTQ+ rights, so to speak: These "special" people are literally and methodically thrown from the tops of buildings, both in Gaza and in other Islamic countries. In Iran, homosexuality is illegal. However, even more ironically, if they agree to be "voluntarily" (surgically and chemically) castrated without any scintilla of regret, they might be accepted in society.

And the irony continues: The only country in the Middle East in which all these types of rights, along with the corresponding thousands of genders and all sorts of enlightened freaks are allowed to exist and celebrate life is... You guessed it: Israel.

However, in the US, pages and pages of "queer studies" are being published, like one particular paper from Duke University, published after October 7, which calls for a boycott of Israel and the now proverbial "freedom for Palestine."

If Lord Jesus Christ were still among us, he would certainly ask his Father to forgive so much ignorance. I, however, was not born to be a sacrificial lamb, nor do I have a good heart: I wish that all these protesters would follow their hearts and move ASAP to Palestine, which they seem to love so much.

The sooner the better.

Good Luck, Antisemites

October 29

Okay, I'm old, but not exactly old enough to have been around during the Nazi era. Nevertheless, today all of us Jews, from my generation and under, are having the privilege of experiencing pogroms, insults, attacks, vandalism, and all kinds of violent racism against Jews...

Ouch, I thought these people abhorred racism in all its forms... But none of that applies to the Jews, right? The Jews are the essence of all evil, a special kind of orange Donald Trump taken to the nth degree and multiplied by, let's say, less than 20 million "units."

The difference now is that, during the pogroms in Russia, the Jews fled to Israel. During the Nazi persecutions, those who were smart fled... to Israel, and to the United States, and even, imagine, to Brazil.

Brazil, once "my" Brazil, which today, with pride, closes ranks with all the other antisemites in the world.

Today, due to Hamas's powerful propaganda machine, endlessly fueled by Iran, the entire world is out in the streets regurgitating antisemitic chants and harassing Jews.

I surrender. There's nowhere to run.

Kill me, if you will, if you believe the world will be better off without me. But before I die, I wish good luck to all the antisemites in the world, who seem to be legion.

Now, take a good look at the human quality of these people who are out in the streets attacking Jews, and prepare yourselves for a "brave new world" in which these people will have the power: Automatons. Brainless. Remote-controlled. I was startled by the look in the eyes of one of those young women who participated in one of the anti-Israel marches this weekend; her gaze was empty, expressionless, like a clueless zombie.

You can already start to say goodbye to technological advances, state-of-the-art medicine, scientific research, ever-improving cell phones, security software, psychology, psychiatry, philosophy, intellectuals, great writers — just to mention a few. You can even say goodbye to artificial intelligence: OpenAI's CEO, Sam Altman, is himself, unfortunately, Jewish.

All of this will disappear, and you will be left with hysterics stoning women and throwing people off the tops of buildings; you will be forced to live with the daily lessons of the ayatollahs on television.

That is, in case there is anyone left who knows how to operate a television, or the internet.

Are they thinking they're going to eliminate the Jews and still preserve modernity?

Think again.

Deluded are those who once believed the end of the world would come from an excess of heat. It will, in fact, come from the absence of Jews.

And when, finally, all of you, the enlightened young, achieve what it is that you want, I, thank God, will be far away, at peace, resting in paradise.

The Era of De-Cultification

October 31

We will only have peace with the Arabs when they love their children more than they hate us. — Golda Meir

On October 6th, just one day before the events that shook our worldview, the hateful Hillary Clinton said in an interview with CNN that "members of the MAGA cult" (a.k.a. Donald Trump voters, "MAGA" standing for "Make America Great Again," an insult to progressives who hate America and, as we can see more clearly now, also hate Jews) should be "deprogrammed."

I wonder if she is wracked with regret right now, but I highly doubt it.

Our topic today, however, is a real cult, a cult of death.

I will make some dangerous statements here today, so anyone who doesn't want to be horrified can stop reading here.

Just stop. Right now.

Much has been criticized, even considering the circumstances, regarding the willingness on Israel's part to eliminate Hamas once and for all as the only way to regain the country's sense of security.

But I'll go even further.

I'm not capable of envisioning these civilians who are victims of this war with pity, nor even condescension.

And why do I say something so awful?

Because, as long as a single Palestinian in the Gaza Strip is alive, we will be in danger, unless they are all... "deprogrammed."

Take this the wrong way if you will, but we all know that Palestinian children are taught to hate Jews from birth, or from kindergarten, and grow up knowing that Israel is a "colonizing" power that "stole" their country, and that all Jews must be eliminated so that they can prosper.

I know the children are not to blame, being subjected as they all are to this constant "programming" and having little access to the real world outside their "hate laboratory." So, what can we expect from them when they grow up?

Every child living in the Palestinian territories today will probably grow up to be an adult capable of killing, and this war certainly is not helping.

One practical result of this "cultification" can be seen in the highly publicized phone call from one of the young Hamas militants who perpetrated the October 7 attacks to his parents, in which he proudly tells them that he had just slaughtered 10 Jews with his bare hands.

His parents, on the phone, treat him like a true hero.

Woe to a world that creates this kind of hero.

Kidnapped

November 1

One of the most depressing, shameful signs of the current capitulation of American society (and other countries) to terrorist propaganda are the people in the streets of major cities tearing up and cursing — yes, cursing — the posters of the victims of October 7 kidnapped in Israel.

The purpose of these posters is obvious: We cannot allow these victims to be forgotten.

We know who these horrible human beings are, preventing the flow of information regarding these more than 230 people — including the elderly, children, and the disabled — held hostage in Hamas tunnels under unknown conditions since the attack.

But who are the people producing these posters?

I just found out: It's a website based in Israel, kidnapped-fromisrael.com, which makes the posters available in several languages for those who prefer to distribute this information, instead of clicking despicable "likes" on TikTok endorsing Palestinian propaganda.

Global posts and views of select hashtags on TikTok

	Views	Posts
Oct. 23-30, 2023		
#standwithPalestine	212m	87k
#standwithIsrael	64m	9k
Oct. 16-23, 2023		
#standwithPalestine	11m	123k
#standwithIsrael	12m	8k

Believe me, you don't want to join forces with these modern-day Nazis.

Posters can be printed and then pasted or distributed anywhere, such as gyms, schools, and universities — especially in colleges, where antisemitic fervor seems to be proliferating like mushrooms after the rain.

Tik, Tok, Tik, Tok

November 2

A newspaper cartoon is often worth a thousand words, and

such is the case with the one published today in *The Times* of London.

In the previous essay, I briefly mentioned a statistic from Axios showing how over 50% of TikTok "users" are against Israel. Over the past 24 hours, the news has spread, with TV showing the actual videos, which perfectly reflect the rhythm of the streets... or perhaps it's the other way around?

TikTok, which began with the innocent posting of short, funny dance videos, has evolved into a powerful propaganda machine in favor of terrorists, and today we are seeing the symptoms of this serious disease spreading in the streets throughout the world.

Don't let yourselves be fooled: TikTok is not a joke; it's a highly addictive drug that is corroding the brains of our youth, who are, by nature, not very inclined to think.

I don't know where all this will end, but I feel the pain. This really hurts.

It's like those ads we see on television here in the US, claiming that "not all people who suffer from alcoholism are addicted to alcohol," meaning that, when one person in your family is an alcoholic, the whole family suffers.

The whole of humankind is suffering.

In an excellent article published today in *The Free Press*, US Representative Mike Gallagher explains this TikTok issue with great clarity, defining the app as "digital fentanyl."

Fentanyl is deadly; just a few micrograms are enough to be fatal, not to mention that it's often mixed into seemingly innocent, yet illegal, opioid pills sold online without a prescription.

You can check out this digital fentanyl on this Palestine Channel on TikTok.

I recommend caution.

Because TikTok, more than a simple digital drug, has ceased to merely threaten all of us with a moral bomb and has entered the countdown to detonation: Tik, tok, tik, tok.

The Great Satan

November 3

You may not be aware but today was a historic day.

After three years of total silence, Hassan Nasrallah, the sacrosanct leader of Hezbollah, gave a live speech in Beirut to offer his "two cents" on the Hamas war.

And what a brilliant piece that was! It put the Third Reich to shame.

I've seen comments on YouTube claiming that Israel missed a "golden opportunity" to get rid of 100,000 enemies all at once (100,000 is the estimated number of people who attended the sacred event in Lebanon).

On the other hand, Israel — which as a result of an enormous effort is now well-positioned in its siege of Gaza City, ready for very dangerous and risky hand-to-hand combat with the enemy — is losing the "public relations war."

Let's face it: Israel always loses the public relations war, perhaps because the hatred of Jews runs too deep in the human psyche for reasons that elude me, or because all the Jews in the world number only a few million, while Muslims number in the billions — the White House has just launched a campaign against *Islamophobia*, probably to help those poor, sparse victims.

But wait, what?

Are they trying to score some points with the ignorant mob, as numerous pro-Palestinian demonstrations are scheduled for this weekend in the US? Because if this is the goal, it's not helping.

The "Great Satan" mentioned in Nasrallah's speech is not Israel, mind you, a country that the "Great Leader" tried to humiliate in his address today by calling it a mere subsidiary of the US. On the contrary, yes, you guessed it: The Great Satan is the United States, and I promise not to blame you if you are unable to sleep tonight out of fear that Hezbollah's bogeyman will come and get you.

I confess I won't be able to sleep either.

And if you think that Israel is the enemy that Hamas is fighting, you are misinformed, my friends. Israel is merely a thorn in their side, an inconvenient pustule in the middle of territories "historically" belonging to the Arabs: This week, the leader of Hamas declared in an interview with CNN (or maybe another channel) that Israel's presence in the Middle East is not "logical," as the legitimate goal, blessed by Allah, is to wipe all Jews from the face of the Earth.

Shabbat Shalom.

***

A brief note: Hezbollah is Iran's terrorist tentacle in Lebanon, whereas Hamas is Iran's terrorist tentacle (but also the local government) in the Gaza Strip. This octopus of evil has other tentacles spread over the Middle East.

A World Without Israel

November 4

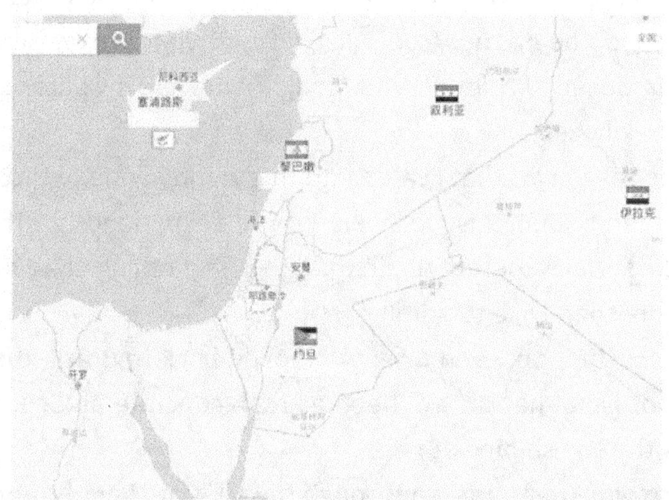

Baidu's "updated" version of the Middle East.

Baidu, the Chinese Google, in a publication today conspicuously failed to identify Israel.

What would happen to me in a world without Israel?

I have complete and total confidence in my country of birth and its armed forces, the powerful IDF. I also have a reasonable degree of confidence in my homeland of choice, the United States — currently one of only two or three countries in the world to openly support Israel.

However, I must confess that, under the current circumstances, the possibility of a world without Israel has indeed crossed my mind, because one can never know. Based on the geographic interpretation of Baidu — the Chinese Google — Israel no longer exists.

My existence is 100% bound to the existence of Israel.

My father met my mother shortly after the War of Independence in 1948, when young Jews from all over the world came together in groups, and a large number of them moved there to work on the kibbutzim, a socialist experiment at the time.

Yes, you heard me: A socialist, leftist, hyper-progressive society, composed of "pioneers." Among them were my parents, who were newlyweds.

The result was that I came into this world in one of those kibbutzim and spent my first year of life "experiencing" this advanced social experiment firsthand — something that marked me more than I like to admit.

From then on, even after we moved back to Brazil, the existence of Israel has always been as real, concrete and certain to me as the sun shining at noon.

Growing up, I suffered through the Six-Day War, the Yom Kippur War, the more recent smaller wars whose names I can't recall — one by one, without ever losing faith.

But never before have I witnessed the horrific scenes we are witnessing now, not limited to the personal accounts, photos and videos of the terrible terrorist attack on October 7, but also including the terrifying social contagion against Jews that seems to have taken over the entire world.

All of this makes me terribly sad. Worse still, it robs me of the courage to go on living.

What would become of me in a world without Israel?

I would probably prefer not to stay alive.

The March of the 100,000

November 5

If just 15 days ago someone had told me that, this Saturday, 100,000 protesters would occupy the streets of DC, and hundreds of thousands more would be marching in the streets of all major capitals of the world, waving green and red flags and shouting "Allahu Akbar," I would have said that person was batshit cuckoo.

But lo and behold, here we are.

"Allahu Akbar" may sound like a loud and contagious call to the crowd of protesters, but make no mistake: This is a religious slogan that bears little resemblance to our better-known "Praise be to Jesus" — normally used to celebrate any kind of joy or miracle — or the Hebrew "Hashem hu Elohim" — "God is our only Lord," where "Hashem" is a substitute word to avoid pronouncing God's name in vain.

Words have power; therefore, one should not trifle with the name of God, much less use it for political manipulation. Right?

Wrong. There goes another traditional truth of the human race rapidly going down the drain, sucked up by social media's infinite capacity for propagation.

Allahu Akbar — in direct translation, "Allah is the greatest" — has long since lost its original meaning as a revelation to Muhammad during a meditation in a cave, having been transformed into the battle cry of jihad, which, in turn, is directly translated as "holy war," whose explicit objective is to delete from this world all Jews, Christians, Buddhists, etc. In short, all the dirty gang of "infidels" who constitute the "rest" of humanity; let him who is thus sinful cast the first stone.

But what kind of God is this, repeatedly praised during unspeakable acts of violence against a fellow human being?

Allahu Akbar has become the preferred soundtrack for the murdering and desecrating of bodies dragged through the streets like lifeless trophies, in inhuman acts of false glory.

Now you tell me: What happened so suddenly to the famous woke saying that "Words are violence," which seemed destined to ameliorate the world and eliminate all differences?

It seems to have instantly vanished from memory in the voices of hypnotized Western youths wrapped in keffiyehs, another traditional symbol bastardized by recent events.

One might even argue that the name of God was invoked in vain in other episodes of violence in the past, such as the Crusades or the "holy" Inquisition in Spain — all historical events pertaining to the Middle Ages, not coincidentally nicknamed the "Dark Ages."

"Dark Ages" was a description of the past coined by the enlightened thinkers of the Renaissance — "Renaissance," for those who don't know it, being historically described as a golden age in which humanity produced philosophers, artists, and humanists, in stark opposition to the piled-up bodies and severed heads so common among their predecessors.

So today, after the Enlightenment, the Industrial Age, the invention of the automobile, the feminist revolution, the space race, and, finally, the glorious advent of personal computers, cell phones, and artificial intelligence, here we are back at the starting point of civilization — "Ground Zero," as we baptized the devastated remains after the attack on the Twin Towers on September 11, 2001.

What a shame, humanity.

Et Tu, Obama?

November 6

In his column this Monday in *The Times* of London, Trevor Phillips — who is black, as if that made any difference — answers a question I had been asking myself and whose answer I already suspected. "I imagine they would be outraged if they were told that their call for justice in one territory might sound to others like an invocation of ethnic cleansing," wrote the columnist, wrongly describing the march as a "group of 40 or 50 women with their baby carriages and some innocuous placards."

The protesters in London over the weekend numbered in the hundreds of thousands, and their placards were far from innocuous, but I always gave them the benefit of the doubt, believing that they didn't know what they were asking for while shouting "From the river to the sea."

However, an article in *The Free Press* written by a 21-year-old Stanford University student shattered my illusions: "Why does my generation hate Jews?"

Good question. Why?

Because all these young people have been indoctrinated in this way since grammar school, and here we are talking about Los Angeles, California, United States of America.

All this empty talk of equality, rejection of racism and acceptance of all differences is simply a lie. Our young people are being taught to hate, and from a very young age.

Contrary to what we have often heard, this is not a "grassroots" movement, or coming from "teachers' unions," or from "queer recruiters," as it may seem at first glance.

All these lies stem from a political desire for power, professed without any scruples by iconic figures in the country, such as, for example... Oh, yes, Barack Hussein Obama.

This weekend, amidst the now-traditional lies about a world on the brink of extinction due to climate change, the beloved "star" of the Democratic Party shamelessly repeated the proverbial lie that the Palestinian land is "occupied."

Even you, Obama?

Occupied by whom?

I refuse to believe that this "guy," who was president of the United States for eight years, is so ignorant about simple geopolitical realities. Well, not so simple, I give you that. But a "literate" and "sophisticated" fellow like Obama should know that what the Palestinians call "occupied" and "usurped" land is neither the Gaza Strip nor the West Bank, no siree.

It is, quite simply, without further ado, the ENTIRE STATE OF ISRAEL. I'll spell it out for you: From the River Jordan to the Mediterranean Sea. And I bet a dollar that Obama knows this very well, or he would be nothing more than just another idiot.

Let's be honest: They want us to disappear from the planet without leaving a trace, but *we* are the ones being called "Nazis."

Smart, Aware

November 7

Much has been said about the possible "reasons" why Jews are so hated.

One of the justifications is that, despite being a minority — which, in theory, should garner some sympathy — Jews tend to be an extremely successful minority, which often arouses the worst feelings in people who can't accomplish anything of value in their own lives, while limiting themselves to hysterically shouting empty slogans in the streets, reflecting the emptiness of their brainwashed minds.

A similar explanation could apply to Asians, who are equally "unqualified" to receive the favor of "equity," so unevenly distributed among the rest of humanity.

I say: Damn those egalitarians from hell.

No one should ever give up on achieving their highest ideals as human beings because of pressure from any of these stupid groups that have recently been gaining prominence.

Regarding this depressing episode of antisemitism on American university campuses — particularly at iconic institutions like Harvard, Yale, Cornell, Columbia, and the like — I was surprised the other day by the eloquence and articulateness of young Jews who are defending themselves publicly, and, in doing so, unmistakably distinguishing themselves from their persecutors.

This is, literally, a confrontation between savagery and civilization, in every observable aspect.

Jews, especially young Jews, are particularly inclined toward liberalism, which includes a constant attack on the Second Amendment every time one of those horrific mass shooting episodes makes the headlines, which is unfortunately common in this country.

There is a persistent refusal by the media and the left to blame the guns, instead of blaming the gun owners, I mean, those gun owners in particular — also known as "criminals" — who have nothing to do with honest citizens who enjoy the constitutional right to own a firearm for their own defense.

Therefore. in light of the recent events, amidst other profound changes being observed in American society in general, mostly toward the rejection of "wokeism," young Jews are changing their minds about the Second Amendment — a transformation I underwent myself as soon as I understood the meaning of the law, or the risk implied by a very dangerous lawlessness.

Smart. Aware.

An Ordeal Difficult to Endure

November 8

I was deeply moved yesterday morning while watching the heartbreaking testimonies of several family members of the hostages, now held in Hamas tunnels for exactly 30 days.

One of them was Doris Liber, whose pain, as promised, I want to share with you today.

A warning: The video available on YouTube is difficult to endure. Mothers will find it even more difficult. Such cruelty!

I don't think we have witnessed a story like this in modern history: over 240 hostages, including women, the elderly, children, and babies, with their families being denied any news of their loved ones.

Thirty days! An eternity for those facing this anguish! All this without any kind of negotiation unfolding; just plain silence.

Last weekend, Secretary of State Antony Blinken visited Qatar, which, in theory, is acting as a mediator. There's only one problem: While "minions" were slaughtering innocent victims and Palestinians are used as "human shields" and "cannonballs" in Gaza, Hamas leadership is enjoying a life of luxury and abundance... in Doha.

I just heard on TV that Qatar was also the mediator responsible for the release of $6 billion in cash to Iran in exchange for five American hostages in September — a negotiation that many envision as underpinning the financial viability of the October 7 attacks.

Can we trust these people?

My hatred grows stronger every day. I never thought I had such a capacity for hating.

I'll finish by quoting Jordan Peterson's post on X, where the psychologist and thinker was intensively targeted for speaking out without any censorship after October 7: Netanyahu, give them hell!

What Are They Afraid Of?

November 9

I'm watching the testimony in Congress of Jewish students who have been receiving threats at universities across the country.

In the middle of a testimony, a pro-Palestinian protester burst into the room screaming hysterically, with a keffiyeh wrapped around her neck and wearing a Covid-type mask on which is written: "Gaza."

I make mental connections immediately, associating different groups of "progressives" and "woke activists" who have one thing in common: denying reality, no matter which reality it might be.

The Covid pandemic ended a long time ago. Vaccine consumption this fall totaled 4% of what was expected. The powerful Pfizer, producer of the most successful RNA vaccine purchased for billions by governments worldwide, is on the verge of bankruptcy.

Why do these people continue to wear masks?

A second after my observations, the TV host makes the exact same comment, speculating that perhaps they don't want to be recognized, but I've already moved on.

The irony of the moment is vivid. Since the pandemic, these masked people have been associated with gagging, and the case of pro-Palestinian protesters is no different: By spreading their belief in Israel's guilt, they simultaneously demonstrate the radical lack of freedom of expression in Arab countries around the Middle East.

In short, the tyrants in charge are all-powerful, while the people are silenced; gagged, if you will.

Who, in their right mind, could be in favor of such a situation?

Only those who, like in Christ's parable, "do not know what they are doing," but don't you expect me to forgive them.

I continue watching the testimonies of young Jewish students being persecuted by antisemitism on university campuses, and behind the young man on the podium I see an elderly woman with a pink bandana that says "Gaza." The tips of her fingers, which are barely visible, are painted red.

Now the irony — or lack thereof — is that these testimonies in Congress do NOT refer to the Gaza war, bloody or not, but rather to antisemitism in American universities, meaning that either these activists don't know what they're doing or know it too well, while stating that "Jews have blood on their hands" and implying a return to the medieval belief that "Jews like to eat little children."

What they want, in short, is for us all to return to the Dark Ages.

No pasarán.

***

I could not end this note without expressing my regret regarding the first fatal victim of these protests, a direct result of the violent pro-Palestinian support being displayed in the United States: Paul Kessler, a 69-year-old man, was peacefully standing on a street corner in Los Angeles on Sunday afternoon, waving an Israeli flag, when he was chased and then struck on the head by a protester.

Kessler was taken to the hospital, where he died last Monday.

The police classified the incident as a homicide but did not go so far as to classify it as a "hate crime," as attested by several witnesses.

Boycott Susan Sarandon

November 9

I arrived home from an incredibly difficult meeting involving life-or-death matters that are not germane right now, turned on the TV, and was immediately taken aback by what I saw.

On the center of the screen, at the podium of a protest in New York City, demanding the immediate release of all Palestinian prisoners of war, was Susan Sarandon, one of my favorite actresses.

As is common knowledge, being an actress in Hollywood is no guarantee of intelligence — quite the opposite. Searching in Google for an image I could use to illustrate the matter, I came across the shocking affirmation that the actress has been on the side of the Palestinians since the beginning of the conflict, and well before that.

There was no mention of the abuses and hideous acts of torture the Israelis were being subjected to, obviously. Only Palestinians matter to these people; Jews are no more than disposable trash.

My God. Human ignorance knows no bounds.

Have you ever thought about the consequences of deciding to "free all Palestinian prisoners"?

Do you know who the Palestinian prisoners detained in Israel really are?

If you don't, I'll tell you: They have nothing, absolutely nothing to do with the poor Palestinian civilians who are victims of abuse coming from all sides. Quite the contrary, they are the most cruel and worst murderous terrorists living in the world right now.

As the British writer and thinker Douglas Murray so aptly put it less than five minutes ago on TV, it would be like releasing all the suspects of terrorism detained in the United States a month after 9/11. But since then, of course, moral relativism has multiplied exponentially with the advent of TikTok and other social media, where, as a rule, the more stupid and outrageous something is, the more clicks it gets.

Please forgive me if you happen to find some typos here. The indignation, in the heat of the moment, didn't allow me to proofread it with the necessary calm.

One thing is for sure: I do not intend to watch another movie with Susan Sarandon ever again.

If no one cancels her, I'll do it myself.

Meanwhile, in Los Angeles, the equally iconic Wonder Woman Gal Gadot, who is Israeli, is being attacked and boycotted in Hollywood, you guessed... for having sponsored the exhibition of I DF footage showing raw scenes from October 7.

Imagine. Even when dying brutally murdered and beheaded you need to be on the "right side" of politics these days.

Barista Mitzvah

November 10

The pun in the title, unfortunately, is not mine, but from the *New York Post.*

For those who don't understand Hebrew or aren't familiar with Jewish traditions, it's a play on words with "bar mitzvah" (the religious coming-of-age ceremony that every Jewish boy celebrates at age 13 after studying the biblical texts to acquire a moral sense), the word "mitzvah" (which in Hebrew means a "sacred duty" we all have to fulfill for the good of our fellow humans), and the obvious "barista," whose meaning I think everyone knows.

The article tells the story of the owner of a New York café, Caffè Aronne, which was about to close its doors after being abandoned by his employees due to his support for Israel — by placing a small white and blue flag at the cash register and displaying posters of hostages in his window… when suddenly, out of the blue, he was saved by the city's Jewish community, which showed up in droves to support him with all its might, facing the dangers that now lurk in the streets of New York for those who display their Jewish identity openly.

Caffè Aronne has enjoyed a permanent waiting line extending around the block since.

I'm a very routine-oriented person, so even amidst the high level of emotion (and degree of improvisation) that has been displayed in these writings, I decided that every Friday I would try to post some good news, which has been so rare in the last 35 days.

But then, as always, reality got in the way.

Last night I couldn't sleep because of too many things rambling in my mind, so at 2 in the morning I gave up and decided to read *The Times* of London. The "article of the day," which already had more than 3,000 comments, was itself a commentary about an article published two days before by Suella Braverman, the UK Home Secretary.

Suella is not Jewish, but of Indian origin like Prime Minister Rishi Sunak himself. Her time in office has been marked by controversy, with a focus on the excessive number of immigrants that is altering the quality of life in England.

In the article, Suella's argument was that the London Metropolitan Police was favoring pro-Palestinian protests instead of focusing on Armistice Day, a crucial celebration for the country taking place tomorrow and being threatened by yet another "jihada day," — sorry, I unintentionally mixed "jihad," which means "holy war," with "intifada," a popular Palestinian uprising that occurred twice in history: the first time in the 1980s, and the second time at the beginning of the 21st century.

According to the *Times*, the original article was even more radical than the version that was published today, as the secretary actually claimed to have "proof" of what she was saying.

Londoners know very well that this evidence exists. While large pro-Palestinian crowds were left alone to celebrate terrorism and shout "Allahu Akbar" as they wished, a few small, localized Jewish demonstrations were systematically repressed by the police.

Because of her chutzpah, Suella is now facing a serious risk of losing her job, under the pretext that she decided to publish it without the mandatory approval of the Conservative Party. The most striking fact, however, is that *The Times* readers overwhelmingly condemned her for causing "division" among the population.

I'm not sure if the paper feels forced to do it, as in recent years the press has been so biased that this has become the "new normal," but *The Times* has been quite neutral since October 7. On the other hand, it is remarkable to see that the majority of readers are openly in favor of the Palestinians — that is, in favor of Hamas, a terrorist group.

Right now, the mob is unanimously demanding Suella's head, and the newspaper is following the heroic saga with a live feed.

I'll leave you with my own comment published in *The Times* early this morning, but I'll spare you the offensive responses I received:

"Maybe what Suella did as a politician was wrong. But as a human being, she was just brave. She saw something, she said something. And what she wrote is 100% right."

Returning to our main topic, if you are in New York today you can celebrate the Shabbat properly and proudly at Caffè Aronne.

Shabbat Shalom.

Cracks in the Ideological Edifice

November 11

Today is Armistice Day, a British holiday that celebrates the end of World War I.

It is also "Veteran's Day" in the US, a day when all veterans of all the wars the country has participated in, living or dead, are honored and celebrated.

Inspiration, anyone?

Instead of reflecting on how British society — and Western society in general — has lost its way and its moral compass, the crowds in the streets of London are vying for space at the Cenotaph, disrupting the traditional tribute to the veterans who saved the world from an unspeakable fate. While demanding attention, the pro-Palestinian mob is also celebrating terrorists and decapitated babies.

Politically charged cartoon by Peter Brookes, published in *The Times* today.

But on this rainy Saturday, I dare to glimpse some signs of hope. (For a gardener, rain per se is always a sign of hope.)

I read so many articles this morning that I can't locate the links, but somewhere I saw two auspicious pieces of news:

1. Israel and Hamas are in talks regarding a ceasefire and the release of hostages

2. Hamas leadership is beginning to show division

The billionaire Ismail Haniyeh, the "political" leader of Hamas who lives in Qatar, is saying that he had no prior knowledge of the October 7 attacks, as are other prominent leaders of the terrorist group, adding that Iran didn't know anything either (which we all know is a lie)

Now, it doesn't really matter if it's a lie and it's obvious to everyone that the attack (allegedly organized by insignificant and unfunded "minions," as I pointed out above), despite its terrible images that will haunt us forever, actually didn't go very well, considering the number of Palestinians who were killed and, I dare say, their imminent defeat in the Gaza Strip.

What's important is that this tragedy changes its tune and begins to draw to a close, which leaves us with an interesting question: What will these millions of people do next, those who have made their antisemitism and racism so obvious, shamelessly joining forces with murderous terrorists?

Will they be able to sleep at night if they ever understand what they've done?

How will they behave when they find themselves abandoned by the professional instigators who led the chanting of genocidal slogans like "From the river to the sea"?

I don't know if it's because I'm a kind of "victim" of these unfortunate circumstances (look at myself already willing to forget about it), but this whole situation seems much more serious to me than, for example, a few beautiful actresses accusing executives of rape 20 years after the facts and other "transformative" movements that, after a few months, fell into oblivion, as if they had never existed.

As I write this note, I see on TV that all hell is breaking loose in the streets of London, a microcosm of the current struggle between civilization and barbarism.

Quote of the Day: Sam Harris

November 12

"Islamophobia is a term created by fascists and used by cowards to manipulate idiots."

They Learned Nothing

November 14

I'll be frank about the radical left: Their revolutions never succeed, their oppressions never end, and their promised futures never arrive. — Os Guinness

The holiday season, whose earliest manifestation is Thanksgiving, is about to begin, and with it, the renewed symptoms of meaninglessness that have infected Western civilization resurge in full force, more like a cancer that starts almost imperceptibly but needs to be eliminated quickly or it will take over the entire organism.

As a friend reminded me the other day, a millimeter of the affected organ can contain billions of cancerous cells, much like a tiny fraction of the American society — the insignificant small town of Wauwatosa, in the state of Wisconsin, which had just banned the use of traditional Christmas colors in holiday decorations on public buildings under the lame excuse that they are not "inclusive" — is yet another sign of moral decay in these times of explicit radicalism.

The curious thing is that, in the report, someone pointed out that these same colors, red and green (minus the black muzzles, of course), are being celebrated by the insane mob that calls itself "pro-Palestinian," shouting their support for murderous terrorists in our streets.

As you know, I'm not a Christian, but I felt like decorating my front lawn with Christmas symbols to demonstrate how this stupid idea of "lack of inclusivity" is one of the least "inclusive" things ever to exist on the face of the Earth, especially considering that Christians are the majority in the US and also in other Western countries.

The problem with these people is that they don't know what they're talking about. These aren't educated people who know their history and how to place themselves within a context, because, after all, educating oneself demands considerable effort, and nobody nowadays is willing to go beyond a few minutes on TikTok — from where, incidentally, their distorted ideas are obtained.

I already raised this point before, when I mentioned that, at some point, Palestinian children would need to be "de-cultified." What I didn't expect was that one of Netanyahu's top advisors would express the same ideas in an interview with Mark Levin last Sunday.

Self-education is essential, so I recommend you take advantage of the opportunity and learn something with the brilliant minds who met in London last week to discuss this exact topic, while extremism was running rampant in yet another battle in the ancient struggle between civilization and barbarism.

Hospitals

November 14

Honestly, I don't understand Hamas's obsession with setting up its headquarters inside hospitals.

What could be the reason?

Hmm.

Perhaps they believe that extending beyond the premise of using residents and civilians as "human shields" would be to, even more boldly, use sick adults, sick children, premature babies in incubators, let's say, as "human shields"?

The media is divided, which is a good sign.

The Times of London, taking advantage of the premise that "a picture is worth a thousand words," opened its article today with a poignant video image of two sad children, remnants of plaster on their faces and arms in casts. Immediately, the article's text proved to be an unnecessary accessory, but readers were not fooled. The comments I read, surprisingly, were overwhelmingly in favor of Israel.

The New York Times, which in the last 30 days has specialized in technical analysis of videos of hospital bombings, went in the opposite direction, stating that "there is substantial evidence that Hamas has been using the hospital for military operations and has built a command center beneath it as part of the Gaza tunnel network."

The hospital in question this time is Al-Shifa, the largest Palestinian medical complex located in the heart of Gaza City. The "Hamas Ministry of Health" continues attempting to sway the media by portraying the Israeli army as a band of heartless thugs attacking hospitals, but it seems that, this time, it's not succeeding very well.

In a speech last night, in English, Netanyahu offered to set up a field hospital to transfer patients and leave to the "peace specialists" the task of dismantling the terrorist network, but his offer — extremely attractive, considering that Israel has the most advanced medicine in the world — simply fell on deaf ears.

Why is that? Could it be that Hamas has no interest in treating its sick?

Hmm.

The medical media campaign suffered an even greater blow with a video that clearly shows bombs and weapons decorating a room in the children's ward.

In a different setting, a few things also seem to be changing. After being exposed to the terrifying images of October 7 — that the IDF is showing to small, select audiences — ceasefire advocates are gradually changing their minds, including the Senate Majority Leader, Chuck Schumer.

In addition to all this, today is an important day: A march is currently in "staging" mode, the very first involving a large audience showing support for Israel in Washington, D.C.

We are actively monitoring the situation.

Our Love Is Bigger Than Their Hate

November 15

The difference was abysmal, obvious to everyone.

One hundred thousand people attended the pro-Israel march in Washington. We've already seen the images from a crowded esplanade.

Instead of hysterical cries calling for ethnic cleansing, there were prayers, traditional blessings, and even a rock band.

Instead of posters calling for "Death to the Jews," there were signs saying, "Our love is bigger than their hate."

Instead of the colors of hell, the colors of heaven.

And that was not all. Anyone who believes only Jews attended the march is mistaken. At one point, on the podium, leaders from both political parties — including the leaders of Congress, Republican Mike Johnson and Democrat Hakeem Jeffries, as well as the Senate leader, Democrat Chuck Schumer — shouted the message, hand in hand: "We stand with Israel!"

It is an illusion to think, based on the noisy pro-Palestinian demonstrations, that this is America's choice. It is not. This is merely the gaslighting of a group of useful idiots backed by a lot of money and radical tendencies from the left.

The American people, united, support Israel.

***

I'll now take a moment to share a personal testimony.

On this day, November 15th, exactly 19 years ago, an event changed my life, or should I say, allowed me to start living my real life: my meeting with Alan on the internet, as a consequence of which you have me writing to you here today.

Alan gave me many things, including this crucial advice: "Want to be a writer? Then start writing every day." I was 52 years old.

So today, I will limit myself to following the advice of one of the college students who spoke yesterday at the pro-Israel march: "Want to save the world? Go home and love your family."

Oppressors vs. Oppressed

November 16

"Oppressed" are peaceful victims.
"Oppressors" are violent.
Right?
Well, not so fast.
In response to the pro-Israel march the day before yesterday, which peacefully gathered 300,000 people in Washington, without a single incident...

...the noble and evolved pro-Palestinian demonstrators put on the spectacle of civility we could all witness in video.

Now, if you decide to check it online, you will see that this note was wrong. The number of participants in the pro-Israel march was 300,000, not 100,000 as I hastily stated earlier. Again, no incidents: just love and peace.

For these and other reasons, I ask you please not to waste your time wishing that I would be "impartial," in the sense of dedicating the same time and effort to both sides of this conflict.

I'm not. I will not. On the contrary, I am unabashedly pro-Israel, and for good reason.

I'm aware of the integrity and firmness of intentions of the Israeli army and government since I was born, and much water has flowed under this bridge since.

I'm aware of the ill intentions and manipulations of Islamic leaders in the Israeli-Palestinian conflict for roughly the same period, and more recently we got evidence enough to reaffirm this, or rather, if we take into account not only the most recent events, but also Egypt's and other Arab countries' emphatic refusal to accept their "brothers in need" in their midst.

Why is that?

Political manipulation above all else, anyone?

***

The other day, afraid of hearing my own voice, I told Alan that I believed the hostages were already dead.

Yes, I hope I'm wrong, totally and completely wrong. But I just heard on TV that the body of one of the hostages, a 60-year-old woman, has just been recovered by the IDF.

The victim in question was a pacifist, a resident of kibbutz Be'eri, and her husband, also murdered with extreme cruelty, was that man we all heard about, who used to enter Gaza to transport sick Palestinians to Israeli hospitals.

Z"L.

As the popular saying goes, "No good deed goes unpunished."

Bin Laden, My Hero

November 17

I imagine many people must have been shocked by my statement yesterday that I'm not interested in listening to the arguments of "the other side," therefore concluding that I'm just as bad and as radical as "them," equally despicable.

Except that... the truth is that few people today dare to call the "other side" radical and despicable.

I do have sympathy for a few Muslim groups — like, for example, the Uyghurs, whom the Chinese government has been sterilizing for the purpose of "ethnic cleansing," while keeping them in concentration camps for years — but I'm not right about this one: In "good society," it is forbidden to criticize anything China does. China is all the rage now, especially in my native Brazil.

I do sympathize with the Palestinian mother who, in despair over her dead son's body, blamed Hamas for her loss, but I'm not right about this one either: In less than a second the reporter turned his back on the poor woman and someone came over to cover her mouth and prevent her from speaking, so don't waste your time looking for this "politically incorrect" story on Google.

I tried. There's not a single mention of it.

There are also some Muslims, whose religion is in the majority, who proclaim themselves to be peaceful, and then there are also the Islamic fundamentalists, who conflate their religion with the state and with the death of all "infidels": me, you, and the entire ROW (Rest of the World).

But, obviously, I'm not the best person to talk about this subject. I recommend that you read, instead, the intellectual and thinker Ayaan Hirsi Ali, a refugee from Somalia who was subjected to genital mutilation as a child and fled to the West, where, after several years protecting herself from a "fatwa," she married the Scottish historian Niall Ferguson and started a family. Both are prolific and easy to find online.

But the central issue I want to address here today is that we are not currently living in normal times, in which we should be kind and understanding toward everyone.

We are at war.

And although many people prefer to think that we're currently witnessing two wars far away from us, one in the Middle East and another in Eastern Europe, these are actually symptoms of a much encompassing reality.

I'll repeat what I've already said over and over, a million times over since I started this series of articles: This is a war for the survival of civilization, a war of good against evil.

You might think we should show compassion toward the oppressed Palestinian people. I'm inclined to agree, provided we switch oppressors: The true and relentless oppressor of the Palestinian people is not Israel, but their own government, not to mention the manipulated data from the "Hamas Ministry of Health," to which I want to devote a specific paragraph.

So it happens that the data from the Hamas Ministry of Health — well respected and widely disseminated without hesitation by the equally respectable mainstream media (or legacy, obsolete media, as some would have it) such as CNN, BBC, and other outlets that many people follow — are a permanently lit fuse whose objective is far nobler and wider than simply wiping off the map that insignificant tripe called Israel, mind you.

On the contrary, they need to eliminate all the infidels and defeat the "Great Satan" — that is, not only the United States, but our whole Western civilization.

The latest episode in this life-or-death war that many still refuse to acknowledge is a "thread" that went viral on TikTok this week, in which beautiful young women of all colors and races, with flawless makeup on, invite you to read a "Letter to America" written by Osama bin Laden, shortly after 9/11.

The infamous Letter to America was rediscovered by some (very) useful activist in the archives of the British newspaper *The Guardian*, but don't waste your precious time looking for it *because*, shortly after TikTok rediscovered it, the newspaper took the letter down.

The language, which is pure poison, explains ISIS's lofty intentions to attack the United States and murder 3,000 innocent people in the most horrific way imaginable, and young American women are now on TikTok with their false eyelashes, winking provocatively while inviting you to read it, learn how to hate America properly and then go out there spreading their moral righteousness.

Which, by the way, is exactly what hundreds of thousands of students are doing right now.

The video doesn't come without a warning about what you're about to find, no siree. "Prepare to have your worldview changed," says the sexy blonde on the screen. "Your life will never be the same again," and she's damn right about that.

If September 11 wasn't enough to finish the job, October 7 certainly was.

Our lives — meaning mine, yours, and the lives of everyone

who is not a fanatical Muslim seeking paradise at any cost — will never be the same again.

Shabbat Shalom.

The Hostages' Dance

November 20

In the early morning hours on Sunday, when Alan was already sleeping, I heard the latest news: An agreement had been reached for the release of the hostages.

The information came from an article in *The Washington Post*, which, unfortunately, I can't link here because, when the sensational information was debunked shortly after, the article vanished along with it.

I can only show secondhand information from one of those news portals that live off food scraps, news alms, if you will. Or I can recommend another article on *Politico*, not about the agreement itself, but about how *The Washington Post* broke the story, raked in some clicks, and later retracted it — that's right, a news portal that writes not about, well, news, but about the story of a news item that never truly became news.

And that's where we are these days.

In other media highlights, the Israeli army (IDF) proved, with a video, that Hamas had taken hostages to the al-Shifa hospital, with the aim, I can only guess, of justifying the "clean-up" they carried out in recent days, demonstrating to the world that it's really true that hospitals in Gaza are more like dens of terrorists than places of healing.

It didn't help much. The self-proclaimed "benevolent" mob continued their noisy demonstrations in favor of the terrorists, the media continued trying to get the scoop regarding the release of the hostages — I just heard on TV that an agreement is close — and, to close the cycle, the UK Home Secretary Suella Braverman remains dismissed, having been fired for telling the truth.

On my end, God forbid, I appear to be losing some of my initial stamina... Well, more or less, or maybe it's just the accumulation of translation jobs I have been waiting for, to which, from now on, I will be forced to devote my attention because the deadlines are approaching.

Life out there goes on unchanged, and the truth is that if we don't hurry — to complete the "destruction" of Hamas, to locate the hostages, to free the hostages, to reach an agreement — the story might be spiked and the media frenzy might go elsewhere, as happened with Ukraine.

Over the weekend I watched a long interview by Lex Fridman with the historian John Mearsheimer (3 hours) in which the interviewee explains how the war in Ukraine could have ended two weeks after it began, saving much destruction and the deaths of thousands, perhaps millions, of young soldiers at this time.

It's a dog-eat-dog world.

We continue to pray for this torture to end soon.

Sophie's Choices

November 21

The issue of the hostages' release agreement is "heating up."

It looks like the long-awaited news is about to burst — oops, I apologize for the misguided metaphor.

What is being speculated is that Hamas will, initially, release 10 hostages to "test" whether the Israelis will actually adopt the ceasefire agreed upon, and then, progressively, other hostages will be released.

The theory is that the elderly, the children, and the disabled will be released first, not necessarily in that order.

Just now I was watching a TV interview with a young man whose 26-year-old twin brothers are supposedly among those detained by Hamas. "My brothers aren't children," he said. "But they are also the children of someone who is suffering."

He went on to say that, since October 7, his life has come to a standstill, and he hasn't been able to function — as a father, a husband, or a regular person.

I can understand what he's saying, I mean, to some extent. I've also been in situations where my life "stopped," and while I had this thought, my eyes filled with tears.

I've been prone to getting very emotional since October 7.

The truth is that nobody knows anything, absolutely anything, about the hostages: where they are, their conditions, how many are still alive and how many have died.

The only certainty is the bodies, like the two bodies found at al-Shifa hospital — two women, incidentally, an indication that, for terrorists, there are no gender or age preferences: All detainees are simply cannon fodder, mere bargaining chips.

The deranged protesters continue shouting "From the river to the sea," a slogan that is gradually becoming automatic and losing its original meaning, something we must not allow to happen. I recently watched a demented old woman — I don't need to be reminded that I'm also a "demented old woman," but with a very different kind of madness — claim that "nobody knows what 'really' happened on October 7." I suggest that New York Governor Kathy Hochul, who is trying to shut these people up, take her aside and show her the explicit images that the general public is being shielded from by the Israeli government.

In another neck of the woods, tonight we are supposed to watch an interview in which Vladimir Zelensky is complaining that, with the war in the Middle East, the war in Ukraine has lost importance, an obvious fact of which we are all aware, but what can we do about it? What a crazy choice is that, between two cruel conflicts, between two different situations in which thousands of people are being sacrificed needlessly?

Certainly, the situation in Israel is taking precedence due to the pressing situation of the hostages, but only God knows for how long.

In an optimistic twist, the journalist who went to Kiev to interview Zelensky is Benjamin Hall, a Fox News reporter who survived his car explosion in Ukraine last March — it feels like a second ago, but not for Benjamin Hall, who lost a leg and his right eye, in addition to several other serious injuries.

Benjamin Hall is a double miracle, the miracle of advanced military medicine in the United States and the miracle of perseverance.

While there's life, there's hope.

Six of Yours for Two of Ours

November 21

"At sixes and sevens," the original idiom I tried and failed to emulate here, means "chaotic, disorganized, in disarray."

What I really intended to do was to share with you the terms of the "fair" agreement about to be approved: 150 murderous thugs residing in Israeli prisons will be released in exchange for 50 hostages.

Who is worth more?
What is the highest bid?
It's pure terror.
And all we can do is wait.

Cancelled!

November 21

After insisting a little longer on her antisemitic drivel, Susan Sarandon was finally cancelled by the agency that represented her, as my note demanded.

I sincerely hope that she goes hungry in her old age (the actress is 877 years old, oops, my finger slipped on the keyboard, of course I meant only 77 years old), and it's high time she retired from the scene with her super corny Disney-themed jacket.

Clearly, she's no longer in her right mind.

Good luck, Susan! I'll be here to remind you of the mess you left when you went away!

The Beginning of the End

November 22

Oyez! Oyez! Oyez!

We've got some news for you this morning. Israel and Hamas have reached an agreement, which was ratified early this Wednesday by the Israeli parliament.

It's not the best thing in the world, but it's a start.

Starting tomorrow, Hamas will release 50 hostages — 30 children, 8 mothers and 12 women — in exchange for a 4-day ceasefire, with the promise that for each additional day of ceasefire, 10 more hostages will be released.

We don't want to fall into the temptation of asking whether this will be the beginning of the end or the end of the beginning.

Understandably, Netanyahu declared in his speech announcing the agreement that "this is not the end of the war," but I sincerely hope it is the beginning of the end, because all wars eventually end with a peace agreement between enemies, or we wouldn't be here today to tell their story.

We are not out of the woods yet regarding the media horrors either. In its edition today, *The Times* of London stated that "the 50 women and children will be exchanged for 150 women and children detained in Israeli prisons."

Excuse me?

I was outraged. I'm sure Israel doesn't keep children imprisoned in "the country's prisons," implying the entire country was one vast penitentiary.

Shortly after, while writing an indignant letter to the newspaper editor (as the comments section, surprisingly, wasn't working this morning), I discovered the source of the story about the imprisoned children in the *New York Post*: "Hamas said in a statement early Wednesday morning that 150 women and children imprisoned in Israeli jails will be released."

Oh, dear. Hamas.

The Times of London goes even further, stating that "most of those detained are serving sentences for throwing stones."

Oh, Hamas. Indeed, a couple of innocent pebbles thrown here and there.

God permitting, we will soon get rid of this damned plague, and I'm not referring to Hamas, but to a Western press that sold its soul to Hamas's "reliable" sources, the evil force behind the millions of people around the world shouting in the streets of major cities, demanding the annihilation of the Jews.

Contrary to what Israeli government spokespersons are saying, I do not endorse the premise that Hamas should be "totally destroyed," especially since we all know that these terrorist organizations are practically impossible to eliminate: when killed here, they sooner or later sprout even stronger elsewhere, like an eternal garden filled with poison ivy.

I'm done with all this.

All I ask is for the hostages to return home, the bodies to be buried, Israel's security to be reinforced, and for this torture to end.

We know it won't be easy to put all this in the past, but the conditions for freedom should not include the total elimination of our enemies; quite the contrary: The price of freedom is eternal vigilance.

Oh, and before I forget, Happy Thanksgiving to y'all!

The Invasion of America by the Arabs

November 23

It's Thanksgiving, a day for eating and drinking our brains out in America, but the pro-genocide activists will not stop.

Yesterday, for example, I had to listen to the outrageous testimony of an "American woman in a hijab"— something that risks becoming increasingly common if we don't act quickly — claiming that the October 7 attacks never happened and that "the Israelis killed their own people," I swear to God — our Almighty host of the day, to whom we give special thanks.

I take this opportunity to share another quote of the day, or rather, the "paragraph of the day" to be honest — yes, I'm also drinking my Single Malt Scotch because I, too, despite being a mere freelance translator, am a child of God: "The mere fact that

Israel is considering accepting such an agreement demonstrates how much Israel cares about the human lives of the people involved. The Israeli negotiators put themselves in the hostages' shoes, imagining how terrible the circumstances must be for them, chained or tied up in dingy underground tunnels for more than six weeks."

In other words: literally risking their lives and the future of the country.

Here in my own hidden cave, I confess I'm eager to get back to writing funny essays and telling you the story of the pressure cooker I bought on Amazon, or how I fell victim to a "job offer" scam that will probably cost me two thousand dollars.

Eeek! Cheers!

Day H, Part 1

November 24

I woke up early and here I am, on standby, awaiting the hostages' release. (Quick note: "H" stands for "hostages.")

One hour to go.

I saw when the ceasefire came into effect before we went to bed and the countdown for the hostages' "delivery" began.

For those of you who aren't following along as anxiously as we are here at home, 13 hostages will be released today.

Thirteen! Out of more than 240! Is this number good luck or bad luck?

Alan — who follows the situation on YouTube more closely than I do, checking several independent commentators — told me something yesterday that I made him repeat more than ten times because I couldn't understand it: He affirmed that Hamas is "in trouble" because **it doesn't know where the hostages are.**

What?

According to Alan, Chuck Holton, a military commentator he follows, said that the terrorists are disorganized and lacking communication among themselves.

Oh. My. God. I hope not; I certainly hope that we won't need to face any more horrors, those poor families.

On CNN right now, I'm listening to a couple who have become very popular. Their son was seen being taken away 49 days ago, after his right arm was blown up and simply disappeared.

They don't know if their son is alive or dead.

I honestly don't know how this mother, Rachel Goldberg-Polin, is holding up. I would have fallen apart a long time ago, but she's still out there, standing tall. She spoke at the UN, she spoke with several world leaders, and she has appeared on various TV channels here in the United States — always calm and composed, drawing strength from I don't know where. She even went to the Vatican and spoke with Pope Francis.

I also saw one of the doctors on the team that will treat the released hostages. Among them, we have just learned, there will be no Americans, although we had previously expected three. He looked anxious, saying that this is not a time for politicians, but for families and for healthcare.

He's absolutely right.

We're following along: another 36 minutes, now 28 minutes, 25 minutes (while I'm rereading this text), assuming that this bunch of animals will be as punctual as a British train used to be.

In exchange for these 13, 39 Palestinians will be released.

Me Too, but Not You

November 25

While we are waiting to see how the psychological torture from Hamas unfolds — some sources are saying that the terrorist bunch declared it has canceled the release of today's "batch" — I leave you with the excruciating video of an Israeli woman recounting a rape concurrent with a murder she witnessed on October 7, manually recorded from my computer's screen.

Along the same lines, *The Times* of London published in today's edition the terrifyingly explicit report from journalist Robert Crampton, who, along with a small, select audience, watched a 45-minute video of the terrorist attack recorded live from cell phones and webcams.

Reading Crampton's report is mandatory, but not for you. All those hysterical young people who continue to be in the streets "demanding" a ceasefire (there *is* a ceasefire in effect at the moment, but reality means nothing to these people), should be forced to watch this video with their eyes held open with pins, like in the iconic scene from Stanley Kubrick's *A Clockwork Orange* (1971).

Midnight in the Garden of Good and Evil

November 25

Five minutes before midnight (local time), after eight hours of unnecessary torture, Hamas handed over its "package" to the Red Cross, in time to fulfill the agreement to release 13 hostages per day.

Technically, five minutes to midnight is still the same day.

Apparently, this morning, upon being informed of Hamas's stalling, Biden picked up the phone and gave an earful to his contact in Qatar, who immediately boarded a plane bound for Israel to resolve the issue.

It's worth remembering that, despite the direct involvement of the US in the hostage rescue, no Americans have been released so far. Among the foreigners (four more were released today), only Thais and one Filipino have been released.

Hamas thinks it holds all the cards, but the truth is that the ill will of Arab countries toward them is growing and their patience is running out.

Day H, Part 2

Good morning.

While we await the liberation of the second batch of hostages, set for the next hour, I invite you to get emotional with me while watching a video showing Ohad Munder-Zichri, the 9-year-old boy genius who was let go in the first batch.

The Times of Israel is publishing moving pictures of families reunited. One image in particular is worth noting: the one showing the Palestinian "children" who were released by Israel yesterday, in which one can see very clearly the difference in the moral standards adopted by the two countries, including the Palestinian "kids" roaring away their appetite for violence.

It is still worth mentioning that today's batch still does not include any Americans. Among those detained is Avigail Idan, the girl whose fourth birthday was celebrated yesterday in captivity.

This must certainly be a provocation. #LetOurPeopleGo

A Climate of Widespread Hatred
Day H, Part 3

November 26

Since today is Sunday, it seems like the suffering is going to take a break.

I just got here and I'm reading in *The Times of Israel* that today's "batch" has already been released, 14 Israelis and 3 foreigners — among them, apparently, Avigail Idan, the 4-year-old orphan girl whose parents were murdered by Hamas on October 7. Avigail has dual citizenship (Israeli/American) and, as I said, celebrated her birthday on Friday.

(Oops, while I'm reviewing this text, Biden is on TV making a statement about it; it seems that "only" the mother was murdered.)

We still have no news regarding the hostages' condition. Yesterday, we learned that one of the young women, who was shot at the event whose name I no longer remember and then kidnapped, went straight to the hospital and will need several surgeries. Her brother, who was at the concert with her, remains in captivity.

From what I've heard, their conditions vary because they were held captive in very different circumstances: some in houses, with access to TV, others in tunnels in total darkness, without even knowing there was a war raging outside.

Before arriving at the office, I read an appalling article by the lawyer Andrea Widburg, whom I like quite a bit. In this text, published today in the *American Thinker*, Andrea compares these terrorists to Nazis, and the terrorists definitely don't look good in the comparison.

You should know that, before October 7, it was forbidden in my "lexicon" to compare anyone or anything to the Nazis, who were, back then, considered as displaying an unreachable level on the scale of evil.

Oh, well. That certainly, like many others, crumbled on October 7.

I've changed. The world has changed.

Among the atrocities she mentioned, Andrea recounts how yesterday, in the West Bank, the mob lynched, hanged, and dismembered two Palestinians — yes, their own compatriots —accusing them, without any proof, of collaborating with Israel. At one point, Andrea says, "one of the executed men had his legs cut off, separated from his body, and thrown onto a pile of garbage."

Later, Andrea shares a video of the sanctified climate activist Greta Thunberg in which the glorified former retarded teenager shouts the slogan along with the crowd: "Let's crush Zionism!"

In Sweden, mind you... an ancient bastion of civilization...

Indeed. The climate on Earth will certainly become much more breathable after the Jews are eliminated and all the world's territories are handed over to Hamas. After all, we can't help but speculate that, behind humanity's unspeakable acts that are destroying the planet, are the usual culprits: the Jews.

Isn't that right?

The proof is in Greta's video.

Have a nice Sunday.

Children with Beards and Mustaches

November 27

Look, I understand the rules of war. I understand that, for these hostages to be released, an outrageous agreement would need to be reached. I even understand the "moral calculations" that for every Israeli civilian released — mostly women and children — three Palestinian prisoners in Israel would need to be returned.

The only thing I don't understand is the need to lie and deceive exhibited by the international media. Even Fox News, which to our utmost relief here at home is about 80% in favor of Israel, fell for this crap and repeated the same tune, incessantly.

On each of the three days of human "exchange" that have taken place so far, the media has overwhelmingly repeated the litany affirming that "Palestinian children and women would be released in exchange for Israeli women and children."

Not a word, of course, explaining to the public that, while the imprisoned Palestinians are all convicted criminals (yes, women can be terrorists as well), the Israeli hostages are all civilians, young pacifists who were participating in a desert rave and entire families surprised in their homes while still sleeping on October 7.

One of the little girls who was released yesterday was still wearing her pajamas.

The "batch" of 14 that we had this Sunday included two families of four members: the mother and three young children, all, of course, with the same last name.

On the other hand, has anyone out there ever seen a child with a beard and a mustache? In the pictures of the released Palestinians, they all have something in common: these are young men with beards and mustaches — which, okay, are traditional in the local culture. Just don't tell me that they're children.

Not one Palestinian child has been seen among the released prisoners so far; maybe, just maybe, because Israel doesn't keep children behind bars.

On the Israeli side, by contrast, we see children, very young children, some under nine years old, some now orphans of both parents... and of aunts and uncles, grandparents, cousins, brothers and sisters — an unprecedented level of orphanhood.

The nursing infants haven't graced us with their entrance yet.

So, for those who don't know what a child looks like, I'm showing you below. At least have the decency to stop lying and deceiving.

Today is allegedly the last day of the truce and the exchange, but Hamas has already stated their interest in extending it. Only God knows how many more living hostages are still available to be exchanged.

Israeli children in captivity in Hamas's dungeons.

Non-Stop Horror

November 28

Dear reader, I know you can't take it anymore. I can't take it anymore either.

But bear with me for a moment and give some thought to the families who are being subjected to this torture without the option of "not taking it anymore."

Yesterday, after the "package" of 11 was delivered — including, once again, an entire family (I mean, almost, because the father remained in captivity), the news was that "a 10-month-old boy — the youngest hostage captured by Hamas — and his family had been handed over to another Palestinian terrorist group," and his relatives are describing the move as "just more psychological torture, fearing that the children are being held as a 'trophy'."

This is Hamas, my friends. I have no words to describe these people.

Kfir Bibas, the 10-month-old baby being "negotiated" by Hamas (family heirloom).

An extra day of truce was extorted from the Israeli government in exchange for another 10 hostages, but we still haven't heard about the "list of the day." Five minutes ago, *The Times of Israel* reported on its live feed that the exchange is scheduled to take place tonight (it is already night in Israel — local time: 6:30 p.m.).

Meanwhile, the "Jewish environmentalists" are expressing their disgust (I'm being kind) for having witnessed Greta Thunberg yell "Let's crush Zionism" at the rally in Stockholm, as we reported the other day — the day before yesterday, to be exact, but it feels as if it was a month ago.

Time passes slowly when we are under the yoke of suffering.

I continue to struggle with myself trying to appreciate Biden's help in this dramatic chapter, but yesterday we heard that, in a "secret" meeting, Biden apologized to the "Muslim community" for having doubted the veracity of the information offered by the Hamas "Ministry of Health."

As the popular saying goes, "light one candle to God and another to the devil."

I'll go back there to throw up and will be right back.

And Even More Horror

November 29

Have you seen those hostages smiling and waving goodbye as they were being released by Hamas?

So, there you have it: Everything is forced; everything is propaganda.

As the number of hostages returning to Israel increases, so do the horror stories.

In this Tuesday's edition, *The Times of Israel* reports that Hamas forced child hostages to watch videos of the October 7 atrocities... all this without uttering a sound. They were conditioned not to make any noise and, to prevent them from crying, had guns pointed at their heads.

Very "well treated" by the terrorists indeed, and yet they were lucky, if compared to several of the remaining hostages who went astray: Nobody knows where they are, something that was officially confirmed this Tuesday.

The curious thing is that, in our Saturday edition — obviously being hyperbolic — I wrote that "all these hysterical young people who continue to be in the streets 'demanding' a ceasefire should be forced to watch the video of the atrocities with their eyes held open with pins, like in the iconic scene from Kubrick's *A Clockwork Orange*." Unbelievable!

While some people are making horror movies using these ideas, these terrorists bring them to life as if it were a walk in the park. Not even the horrific treatment of American prisoners of war by the Japanese in World War II comes close to this level of cruelty, not to mention the Nazis — neck and neck.

The 9-year-old Irish girl who was released on Monday, Emily Hand, told her father that she believed she had been in captivity for a year.

Meanwhile, Israel pledged to release 50 women during the extended truce, including two convicted criminals and one accused of attempted murder.

I highly doubt that the explicit nature of these accounts we have already heard, and those we will certainly hear in the near future, will do anything to melt the hearts of any of these hysterical protesters: Have you noticed that most of the cries of "Free Palestine" are in fact voices of hysterical women?

Why is that? Do these women admire the near-captivity state in which every woman in Gaza lives?

And speaking of hearts, commenting on the fact that dead Israeli soldiers donated their organs and saved the lives of several people, Alan told me that the same thing was happening on the terrorists' side, except for the hearts... because they have no hearts.

Meanwhile, we learned that even the corpses of dead Israeli soldiers were kidnapped on October 7, because the terrorists know that the body of an Israeli soldier is worth its weight in gold... as a "bargaining chip."

All of this can be followed minute by minute in *The Times of Israel* live feed, but on this Tuesday evening, while I'm preparing tomorrow morning's edition, there is an unsettling silence of more than two hours.

Earlier today, Hamas broke the truce and attacked Israeli forces resulting in several injuries, so the future of the now routine "truce & hostage exchange" pair might be in danger, even if a potential "10-day window" has already been agreed, which, in theory, would resolve the vast majority of hostages.

As a glimmer of hope, the foreign ministers of G7 countries — Canada, France, Germany, Italy, Japan, United Kingdom, and United States — together with the High Representative of the European Union, are demanding the unconditional release of all hostages.

It's high time that the decent leaders of this world put an end to this.

Sorrow Never Ends

November 29

I had planned a productive day, waking up early and starting to work right away, but "heigh-ho, here we go!"

I started by checking *The Times of Israel* feed and came across the tragic news: Hamas informed the IDF that the "red-haired family" including 10-month-old Kfir — shown in a family picture on Tuesday's entry — his 4-year-old brother Ariel and their mother Shiri Bibas were not in fact with another terrorist group. They had been murdered by Hamas.

Just like that, as if it were nothing.

What Hamas says is not gospel, but in this case, either it's true (*The Times* said the report was unconfirmed) or, even if they are alive, these three got lost in Gaza.

One way or another, Hamas's cruelty seems endless, a bottomless pit whose bottom, it looks like, will never be reached.

Please forgive me if I address each hostage by name and as if they were a close relative: That's because they really are.

It feels as if, since October 7, every time the sun comes up, I lose a close relative.

It's been 54 days.

How to Leave the Entire American Senate Speechless

November 30

As I write this, I have no news of any extension of the truce. Yesterday was the last day agreed upon, with ten hostages released at the end of the day, several hours after two Russian hostages with dual nationality were let go.

The near future is uncertain, but it's quite obvious that nobody can stand this piecemeal "justice" any longer. And it's also out of proportion.

But what I want to share with you today is yet another effect of that famous 43-minute film about October 7 atrocities we've discussed several times here, which is gradually silencing and destroying the defenses of the select groups invited to watch it.

Last week the group included journalists from *The Times* of London. Yesterday, it was the turn of the American Senate.

According to the article in *The Times of Israel*, after watching the video, the senators left the plenary in silence and with tears in their eyes — a crucial moment for Israel, which depends on the US to continue its efforts to eliminate Hamas and, of course, free the remaining hostages.

According to the calculations, there are still one hundred and eighty-something more to go.

I don't know if the UN Secretary-General has already watched the video, but, this Wednesday, António Guterres decided to require a thorough investigation into the "alleged" sexual violence perpetrated against Israeli women on October 7, something he considers unacceptable.

Only 55 days have passed.

Negotiating Bodies

November 30

When it comes to Hamas's captives, they are not all Jews. Besides the several Thais who were already released and the Russians with dual citizenship — according to the monsters, released to "please Putin" — we also have, believe it or not, Arabs, or rather, Bedouins, like the brothers Aisha and Bilal Ziyadne, captured along with their father, Youssef, and older sister,[4] of whom nothing has been heard since.

One new extension of the truce was hastily negotiated yesterday, after the release of the 12 hostages, but today the tone has changed, as, in addition to the eight people already promised, three bodies will be "freed."

Yes, you heard me. Hamas is "charging" for returning dead bodies.

One of the most painful aspects of this hostage situation is that most families have no idea about the health status of their loved ones, where they are, and of course, in the case of these cruel animals that are part of Hamas, whether they are alive or dead.

---

[4] A fact check while editing this book (February 2026) informed that it was not an older sister who was captured with the Ziyadne family, but and older brother, Hamza.

Today, this suspense will come to an end for a few families that will receive their dead back. Once this has started (I mean, the release of corpses), we don't know when it's going to stop.

There is no life left.

It's the end of all hope.

A Cattle's Life

December 1

Mia Schem, 21 years old, was released this Thursday.

Alive.

Mia's mother waged a fierce campaign in the American media on behalf of her daughter's freedom.

She was rewarded.

Mia arrived with her arm in a cast. She was shot at the music festival where she was abducted 56 days ago and, according to her own account, underwent surgery "performed by a veterinarian."

She's lucky that Israeli medicine is very advanced and will certainly find a way to fix it, whatever it is.

Mia will have a future.

Young Yagil, 12, and his brother Or, 16, will be marked forever, and I'm not talking about the psychological damage, which I'm not even capable of assessing: both were branded on their legs, like cattle, on the exhaust pipe of a motorcycle, so that "Hamas could find them if they tried to escape."

The boys' uncle, who was "returned" earlier this week, told us that some of the stories his nephews told him were terrifying. All the children were marked in a similar way, frequently abused, and constantly drugged.

At least Yagil and Or are now free.

And alive.

Others might not be so lucky.

Yesterday, just minutes before midnight — in psychological warfare, every minute is precious —Hamas handed over a "package" containing only six hostages. Two Russian women were released earlier, and for the brutal animals they are, Hamas's bookkeeping is quite rigorous: The commitment for this extended truce is to release 10 hostages per day, but, as there were 12 on Wednesday, the two extra hostages were duly deducted from today's quota.

Among them were the Bedouin siblings we highlighted in yesterday's edition.

Alive.

They have a future ahead of them.

God willing, they will be able to live on without prioritizing their trauma.

All the other men, including fathers, brothers, and husbands, remain in captivity, with no prospects at the moment.

Among the children, from what I could gather, only the two boys from the Bibas family are still missing: Kfir, 10 months old, and Ariel, four years old, precisely those whom Hamas claims were killed, along with their mother Shiri, by an "Israeli forces bombing."

When this edition went live, the promised return of the bodies had not yet been confirmed.

Protester on Fire

December 1

We've already mentioned here that the world seems hypnotized, possessed by an evil spirit whose origin is unknown — to some extent.

Perhaps the devil exists and is on the loose.

Perhaps we are simply witnessing another episode of "the banality of evil."

Perhaps it's just another symptom of the moral sickness that's widespread on social media; who knows?

Until now, it seemed that the only ones at risk of becoming victims of this collective hysteria were us, the Jews. But today, things have changed a bit.

Please understand: The entire world seems to be in danger and out of control because of this widespread madness. On Friday afternoon, beside herself, a protester wrapped in a Palestinian flag set herself on fire in front of the Israeli consulate in Atlanta. She's now in the hospital in serious condition.

She must have thought, obviously with an entirely skewed intensity, that the situation in Gaza was — for her, an American citizen — as serious as that of the Buddhist monk who immolated himself in Saigon in 1963, in protest against the Vietnam War.

The monk was an idealist and became immortalized because of it. He has my respect. But today's protester is just another useful idiot, a victim of political manipulation who has lost all sense of proportion.

Like everyone else, I'm anxious for this war in Gaza to end, but it wasn't Israel that took the initiative to break the ceasefire. Just like after October 7, it was Hamas that took the initiative to attack.

If you think I'm going to get emotional over this insane person's reckless act, think again. This is simply a psychiatric nutcase, totally deranged.

Call me insensitive, if you like. I don't really care.

Shabbat Shalom.

Only Eternal Victims Are Good Enough

December 3

Watching Alexandria Ocasio-Cortez rambling on TV just a few minutes ago, I found myself asking, for the zillionth time, why the progressives and leftists of this world — whom I have come to fervently detest throughout my life — are so unanimous in their condemnation of Israel.

From a Manichean point of view, it's easy to understand: These people love a nice victim — those incapable of defending themselves, those who depend on the favor of their charitable souls to survive.

Seen in this way, Israel is, in effect, the stronger side of the rope, if we consider the following:

- It is one of the most advanced democracies in the world, and the only one in the Middle East.

- It is an undisputed global leader in terms of technology and medical advancements.

- Its secret service, the Mossad, is legendary for its efficiency.

- And, finally, its army is considered the most powerful in the world — not to mention that, although it doesn't explicitly declare it, tiny Israel is an honorary member of the nuclear club.

Who could love a country so clearly successful and self-sufficient?

Obviously, it wasn't always like this. Just over 75 years ago, a group of survivors of the Second World War left Europe to start a new life in the Middle East — a place considered sacred to Jews since biblical times and, probably, well before that.

In a scene from Kenneth Branagh's wonderful new film, *A Haunting in Venice*, the frail doctor tells Hercule Poirot what the nature of his illness is.[5] In 1945, at the end of World War II, he was among the soldiers who liberated the Bergen-Belsen extermination camp. The doctor describes to the detective in detail that the place was infested by rats, the huts so badly covered in mold that they had to set them on fire, not to mention the rescue of the "skeletons," and ends by recounting how, acting with the best intentions, he had killed two former camp inmates by giving them a glass of milk (feeding a severely malnourished human being too quickly can indeed be fatal). After witnessing all this, the good doctor tried to commit suicide by shooting himself in the chest.

These were the people with numbers tattooed on their arms who arrived in the British protectorate called Palestine from 1945/46 onwards, several of them aboard the iconic ship *SS Exodus*, planning to create a new life for themselves.

The day after the UN declared the creation of Israel in 1948 (we are aware of the irony in light of UN actions today), the tiny territory and its improvised army, with very few weapons, were savagely attacked from all sides by their new Arab neighbors determined to eliminate them.

---

[5] The film is based on Agatha Christie's novel Hallowe'en Party, published in 1969 as part of the Hercule Poirot series.

I don't need to tell you that Israel won the War of Independence due to the sheer bravery and intelligence of its non-soldiers, or we wouldn't be here today to tell this story.

With this victory, they had earned a country that was mostly an arid desert, now literally transformed by the workings of their strong will into a "land of milk and honey."

It is true that Israel has a powerful ally in the United States, but their life story makes it very clear that the people who live there are highly capable of overcoming adversity, regardless of the severity and precariousness of their initial conditions.

Unfortunately, this world's keepers of justice do not appreciate this kind of independent spirit; they prefer the eternal victims, eternally piled up like garbage in the worst rat's nests on the planet — and this is not meant as a criticism of the citizens of Gaza, but rather of those who strive to keep them firmly oppressed under the yoke of eternal misery.

As a brief consolation, on Friday Susan Sarandon made a sort of *mea culpa* as she publicly apologized for her harsh words related to Jews — one of the few media figures, in this era of extremism we are facing, to retract their antisemitic attacks.

But don't let yourselves be fooled: The famous actress only did this because she was fired by her agent and is currently unable to work. The owner of her talent agency, unfortunately for her, is also Jewish.

A Jewish Voice Arises

December 5

I was pleased today by the video of a press conference with House Speaker Mike Johnson, which included highly articulate testimonies from Ivy League Jewish students regarding the wave of antisemitism on campus.

We could describe it as "history being written live."

I share with these students the idea that I don't want to be here writing about these things, because that's not my job. My job is to write weekly funny, ironic essays about everyday absurdities.

Or at least it used to be.

The current state of war has profoundly transformed the daily lives of our community, in the United States and the rest of the world.

The presidents of (formerly) important universities like Harvard are now testifying before Congress and stumbling while trying to justify their indifference.

According to the president of Harvard at this very moment, "words are not violence" — the exact opposite of the woke philosophy which posits that, well, "words are violence."

It is in fact history being "rewritten live," according to the convenience and without the slightest shame!

Sex and Money Crimes

December 6

This is from CNN, which I mention purposely, so you can see that today, sixty days after the October 7 attacks, some terrifying truths are beginning to come to light, and yet the truth-deniers continue on.

Let's start with money, which is more, shall we say, "palatable."

Today's news highlights the fact that Hamas includes in its ranks financial market experts who made billions of dollars in profit selling shares on the Israeli Stock Exchange with insider information about the attacks, after which the stock market obviously crashed.

This is something we could call, without fear of being wrong, "blood money."

The other issue, the sexual issue, is the refusal of certain activists, including Briahna Joy Gray — a former spokesperson for Bernie Sanders, who himself is Jewish — to accept the all-too-obvious fact that Israeli women were victims of horrific sexual abuse before being murdered on October 7. In her thread on Twitter,[6] Briahna argues that movements like #MeToo, with their decree to "Believe all women," have always been an exaggeration, and concludes by saying that there are no testimonies from the victims.

Well, of course not! They are all dead!

Furthermore, the Israeli government presented over 1,500 pieces of evidence of extreme sexual violence, collected from witness testimonies, videos from terrorists' cell phones, and the remains of victims.

In a statement released Tuesday, the State Department noted that one reason why Hamas interrupted the release of the hostages and consequently broke the ceasefire is that they don't want the released women to tell the world about the abuses they suffered.

The curious thing is to observe that the most stubborn activists have their public days numbered, because the mainstream media, including CNN, PBS, MSNBC and others, as well as traditionally "progressive" programs like the odious *The View*, are overwhelmingly condemning the lack of condemnation.

------

[6] When this entry was written, in December 2023, Twitter's new identity as X had not yet begun to "sink in."

Even Hillary Clinton, whom I generally dislike, gave a striking testimony. Since the war began, in fact, I have mostly agreed with Hillary Clinton in every way, shape, and form.

Among all the voices I heard, I hand-picked for you the testimony of Sheryl Sandberg — the famous feminist and former powerful Facebook COO — at the UN pro-Israel event on Monday.

Stupidity Has No Gender, Nor Color.

December 6

No one has said it yet, so I will: The three presidents of some major Ivy League universities I mentioned in my note yesterday are, in fact, three women presidents. Women, all three of them, although most certainly ignoring what a woman is.

The level of hypocrisy of these women, all repeating leftist slogans in unison and, apparently, afraid of "going beyond" the party's guidelines, was jaw-dropping.

Even under intense pressure from Representative Elise Stefanik, they proved incapable of expressing an honest opinion regarding the violent wave of antisemitism on university campuses which, contrary to what Harvard President Claudine Gay said, clearly crossed the line between "speech and conduct."

If asked about the Holocaust, Gay would probably feel compelled to analyze the cremated bodies before offering her "educated opinion."

Even more astonishingly, any theoretical condemnation of antisemitism was rigorously accompanied by a condemnation of Islamophobia, as if the two phenomena were Siamese twins joined at the head.

Of course I don't believe, as my title might suggest, that women are less intelligent than men, or my argument that I myself am an intelligent person wouldn't hold up, and I could be accused of hypocrisy.

However, this is not the problem we face here.

The problem is elevating people to positions of prestige not because they are capable or experienced, but because they belong to one or another "minority" group and, by occupying these positions, will certainly leave their institutions "looking good."

In the case of Claudine Gay, as a Black woman she is twice "qualified." Or not at all.

For a long time now, we have been forced to eat crow and accept these obvious injustices and flawed conceptions that are destroying our society from within.

This wave of antisemitism and the violent glorification of murderous terrorists is "only" the most recent manifestation of this state of affairs.

I hope it will be the last.

Many people are demanding that these three "women presidents" resign in view of their explicit inability to hold their respective positions, which obviously is not helping our cause.

What is in fact helping is that the biggest donors to these universities, shocked by what has been financed with the money they gave away, are withdrawing their contributions.

Harvard, surprisingly, is proving to be a role model for this behavior... of racism, ignorance, and superficiality. To make matters worse, it has also become a breeding ground for antisemitism, even though many of the country's top lawyers who are Harvard graduates are Jewish — I am forced to say.

An Arab Utopia in the Middle East

December 7

I'm not quite sure why, among so many videos I have saved to watch during my "daily session of study" — that is, while working out on the stationary bike — I felt compelled to choose an interview by Jordan Peterson with "His Excellency" Saeed Al Nazari, according to Wikipedia the president of a "Global Happiness Organization" — two important entities I had never heard of until today.

I also can't start to imagine why Peterson chose His Excellency as the interviewee of the week on his Daily Wire channel. Probably Peterson and I — oh, the supreme pretension! — were driven by the same impulse: the need to compensate for almost 100 consecutive days of watching Islamic monsters torturing, slaughtering, and being praised in hysterical genocidal chants, not to mention the piles of rubble that the Gaza Strip has become.

It's easy to conclude that all Muslim Arabs are, at the very least, despicable people, but it wasn't always that way.

Muslims and Arabs once ruled the world, with the Ottoman Empire, for example. They were the pinnacle of culture and science. They were the ones who disseminated the concept of zero, while also being a dominant force in the world of numbers. Have you ever heard of Roman numerals (now generally retired) and Arabic numerals (now immortalized)?

Yeah. You got the idea.

Traditional Islamic architecture has wonderful examples as well, among them the Alhambra Palace in Granada, Spain. Not to mention the poetry of Rumi, considered one of the most inspired in the history of the world.

And then we have the Moor of Venice, Othello, the moral champion in Shakespeare's play of the same name, although some argue that Othello was not a Muslim, but a Christian — something that is not very clear in the play.

Therefore, what the hell happened?

I am not in a good place to analyze why a formerly mesmerizing Arab culture has degenerated into gangs of murderers, but I'm aware that the Emirates, as His Excellency states in his interview, are in fact different.

I recognize that the interview wasn't very good. His Excellency dodged Peterson's most challenging questions, which, if answered, would have been the most enlightening.

I know that many people (me not included, but only as a matter of aesthetic preference) admire Dubai's utopian architecture, and the city is now one of the most popular tourist destinations in the world. I'm also aware that they have a great airline, Emirates. With a little extra effort, I could almost believe that women enjoy freedom in what seems to be a materialized Arab utopia.

However, what I do feel inclined to say — because it's true — is that the Emirates were among the first Arab countries to accept the Abraham Accords — conceived by Jared Kushner, Trump's son-in-law, and which, until a few days before the October 7 attacks, seemed to be an original, solid, and reliable path toward peace in the Middle East.

Today, unfortunately, they are little more than another failed utopia.

There was much speculation in the sense that the reason behind October 7 was that Saudi Arabia, another Arab country that seems to be courting modernity, was about to sign an agreement with Israel, but, as it turned out, the attack started to be planned much earlier.

I'll go even further and venture to say that there is an important distinction between the Arab countries of the "utopian side" and the Arab countries of the "savage side": the willingness to reach peace with Israel.

Perhaps the members of the first side are reaching the end of their patience and preparing to somehow eliminate the other side — which poses an obstacle difficult to overcome in their ambition to become part of the civilized world.

A person has the right to dream.

Better Times Will Come

December 7

For those of you who don't know, Hanukkah is the story of a miracle.

I'm not a storyteller, but you can check out the Wikipedia entry, which is interesting for two reasons: it recounts the miraculous victory of a small heroic people against their imposing rulers and includes the following statement: "In the year 200 BC, the Jews lived as an autonomous people in the land of Israel."

So, there you have it.

It's been a long time, and we're still here.

When these terrible times are over, we will still be here.

You can count on it.

Happy Hanukkah!

The Resounding Failure of Leftist Ideology
A Point of No Return

December 8

It seems that genocide and antisemitism are "the women" of the moment.

Asking can't hurt: Why does the left seem so lost on the most basic issues?

Shabbat Shalom.

64 Days

December 9

A few days ago, Hamas published a propaganda video intended to torture families into pressuring the Israeli government, showing the state of mind of three hostages on the 23rd day of their captivity.

As the title of this note shows, we are on Day 64.

What happened to them? Although most of the women and children have been freed, 17 women and two children remain, one of them a 10-month-old baby.

I'm not entirely sure if the two children are included on the list or not, or if they are alive or dead, as I haven't been able to find accurate, up-to-date information.

This is what happens with very prolonged wars: The "freshness" of events turns into stale bread, the surprise wears off, the shock cools down, people get used to the hardship, and the dramatic events happening beyond our close neighborhood end up being forgotten.

The same has happened with the war in Ukraine, which is only mentioned when, from time to time, the government tries to convince Congress to release more money.

I came across this video through a link on a terrifying article published yesterday in *The Free Press*, written by Naama Levy's mother — Naama being the woman who appeared in a Hamas video the day after the attack, with bloodied pants and "ankles cut so she couldn't run." Who had ever heard of such a thing before this horrific war?

In the article, whose translation I'm trying to negotiate, Ayelet Levy says the following: "The 17 female hostages are not bargaining chips to be debated by diplomats. They are someone's daughters, and one of them is mine."

Ayelet has not heard from her daughter for 64 days.

Sporadic news reports casually indicate that this or that hostage has been killed, "before or after the kidnapping," and that the Israeli government is claiming their bodies. I just heard on TV that 17 victims have already been declared dead. (I'm not entirely sure about that number either.)

Yesterday, at a UN Security Council meeting, the United States safeguarded Israel's right to self-defense by vetoing a resolution that would have forced the country into a ceasefire. The resolution was rejected with 13 votes in favor, one abstention (UK) and one against (US).

A ceasefire, as we have already discussed here extensively, favors Hamas. Israel claims it will need at least two more months of fighting to end the "first phase" of the war, which consists of dismantling Hamas.

Where will we be in two months? Where will the hostages be? Where will Naama be?

Nobody knows.

Meanwhile, everything we hear on the news — that Hamas uses hospitals and schools as military bases, about the network of tunnels, the thousands of people who are dead or have been displaced, and, last but not least, the hostages who have not been released — is beginning to take on a feel of *déjà vu*.

We cannot allow this to happen.

Kindergarten of Terror

December 10

Many people doubt Israel when the IDF says that Hamas uses hospitals, schools, daycare centers, and UN facilities to hide terrorists and conceal weapons and ammunition.

One of the differences between Israel and Hamas is that Israel proves what it says, as shown in the video released yesterday showing, well, weapons and ammunition inside a teddy bear.

Cute, but not that cute.

Innocent civilian victims, but not that innocent.

A Light at the End of the Tunnel...
...and I Hope it's Not a Train

December 10

More than 150 Hamas terrorists surrendered to the IDF in Khan Yunis, south of Gaza.

I don't need anyone to tell me.

I am aware that the tone of these notes has been extremely pessimistic, and for obvious reasons.

But it's difficult to live with extreme pessimism for a long time, unless you suffer from clinical depression, which is not my case.

So, I'm scouring the news for a little relief, even if it's just minimal.

Yesterday, the IDF informed they have begun to perceive signs of a breakdown in resistance among Hamas terrorists (yes, we refuse to call them "militants" or "soldiers," terms reserved for nobler causes than the pure and simple extermination of Jews). One of these "signs" is the beginning of a wave of capitulations, with the release of images like the one above.

According to figures reported by Hamas's "Ministry of Health" (because we have no other sources), more than 17,000 Palestinians have already died in this war, most of them "women and children." Of these, the IDF estimates that 7,000 are terrorists: a good "cleansing," not ethnic, but moral.

Our hope is that, God forbid, we won't need another Hiroshima for the surrender to be total and unconditional.

Another positive sign was the resignation of UPenn's president Elizabeth Magill, even if it didn't happen because she "came to her senses" after her disastrous testimony before Congress last week, but rather because the university's largest donor, with a pending donation of $100 million, made her resignation a condition for releasing the funds. The president's "decision" didn't take long to be made, as the implications — financial, not moral — were obvious.

Further resignations are expected throughout the week, according to Clarice Feldman's column published this Sunday in the *American Thinker* under the inspired title "Dumb, Dumber, Dumbest," which I highly recommend.

In the article, similar to what I have done, Clarice associates the stupidity of the students — who, I must clarify, were about 90% of the participants in the pro-Palestinian demonstrations that now seem to have "cooled down" — to some of the idiotic mandates from the "woke era" we have been subjected to, such as, for example, the "pronoun policies" that make absolutely no sense.

A curious fact is that one of the arguments raised by the presidents of UPenn, Harvard, and MIT in Congress is that, if penalized, the university would lose its primary source of international students who would possibly lose their visas, a considerable percentage of whom come from Qatar, the country that is the "headquarters of the negotiators" but also, surprisingly, the biggest Hamas's financer — speaking of conflict of interests.

In short, the October 7 attacks were a trigger, but the underlying causes have been brewing for a long time — most notably at these elite universities that are famous worldwide.

I'm hoping this unsavory mix will soon boil over.

However, the "touch of hope" I was referring to was not the stupidity of the protesters, but rather the fact, clearly stated in Clarice's text in unequivocal percentage terms, that the students had no idea of what they were saying: once informed of what the slogans really meant and after observing a map of the region that was shown to them, most simply changed their minds about their loyalty to terrorists.

It could be the beginning of an auspicious turnaround.

Dreaming is free.

Have a nice Sunday.

Weights Without Measures

December 11

The main topic of discussion among commentators over the weekend was whether the university presidents should resign or if all these episodes of pro-Palestinian demonstrations were simply a matter of "freedom of speech."

What's that popular saying again, "One person's freedom ends where another's begins," or something like that?

Others came to the same conclusion as I did, namely that this would be the beginning of the downfall of the entire "woke" edifice.

A good summary of the debate can be read in *The Free Press*. Among the articles, one historical account written by Niall Fergusson presents a topic that has also been raised elsewhere, recalling how German universities were favorable to Hitler in the 1930s. Nazism, as Fergusson points out, was obviously responsible for "elevating" the universities in the Unites States as a preferred destination for the widespread "brain drain" caused by the persecution of Jews.

Interestingly, it seems that these people who are ardently defending Hamas, including the October 7 attacks, are preaching to a choir but hitting a sour note.

For example, according to Yousef al-Mansi, the former Hamas minister of communications allegedly being interrogated by Shin Bet, "this is a group of crazy people that Sinwar leads. They destroyed the Gaza Strip. Set it back 200 years. People in Gaza say that Sinwar and his group destroyed us. We need to get rid of them."

Yahya Sinwar is considered the mastermind behind the October 7 attacks. His "residence" in Khan Yunis is the apparent reason for IDF's presence in the southern Gaza city.

The death or capture of Sinwar, combined, of course, with the return of all hostages — including the dead ones — would potentially put an end to this war.

Biden: "I Am a Zionist"

December 12

In difficult times like these, every bit of support is precious. But when this support comes from the president of the most powerful nation in the world... enough said.

As the Psalm goes, "I wash my hands in innocence and go around your altar, Lord."

We have fought the good fight; now let's keep the faith.

Fetterman Saw the Light

December 13

The other day I asked Alan, "Hey, what happened to John Fetterman? He stopped being a retard and everything he's saying now sounds like the voice of reason."

For those who still don't know him, John Fetterman is a Democratic senator from Pennsylvania who was elected last year, built like a monolith and, by the way, married to a Brazilian. Shortly before the elections, the future senator suffered a stroke that notably affected his speech and his ability to understand.

Fetterman finished his campaign and participated in the debates with the help of a computer, which was painful to watch.

He was elected anyway. "It's the corruption of the Democratic Party," was the general comment from "our" side of the political spectrum.

In the plenary sessions, he refused to wear a suit and tie and always appeared wearing shorts, flip-flops, and a hooded sweatshirt that made him look highly suspicious.

Due to progressives' obsession with "protecting" the disadvantaged and the ones in need, the Senate passed a resolution allowing each senator to dress as they pleased (before that, formal attire was mandatory). It was a complete disaster, and two days later, the resolution was canceled.

Shortly after taking office, Fetterman was hospitalized for severe depression and spent four months in the hospital, unable to work. Throughout this time, he was a prime target for Republicans, who used the occasion to point out the level of absurdity that had taken hold of progressives and the Democratic Party.

Surprisingly, after October 7 Fetterman started making declarations that flatly contradicted his progressive colleagues, in strong support of Israel and the Jewish people, and he hasn't stopped since.

Everything the senator says is now absolutely correct, not "politically" correct — a notion that, according to Konstantin Kisin, was created in the Soviet Union to throw the enemies of the state into the Gulag.

But why am I wasting time and energy talking about these things when so many serious events are happening?

Yesterday, the UN General Assembly overwhelmingly approved a resolution forcing Israel to accept a ceasefire, although the resolution is "non-binding," meaning it's not worth the bits in which it was saved

The IDF reported that it has begun to flood the Gaza tunnels using seawater — a controversial strategy, especially considering the fear that some hostages might be in those tunnels, but I remain confident that the IDF knows what it's doing.

After the October 7 attacks, the distribution of forces and opinions seems to be shifting. It no longer matters whether you belong to the left or the right, a dichotomy that has long since ceased to have meaning. The edifice of opinions has undergone a radical shrinking and has been reduced to a single factor: whether you are for or against Israel.

I don't have a shadow of a doubt regarding where I stand, which is kind of reassuring.

The Fallacy of International Kindness

December 15

"On Simchat Torah it became finally clear that there is no God; on Hanukkah it became finally clear that there are no miracles," reads a comment from an Israeli woman posted on social media yesterday.

Who in their right mind can possibly cope with this?

For those who don't know, Simchat Torah is the Jewish holiday that commemorates the end of the annual Torah reading — a celebration of God's existence. In 2023, Simchat Torah fell on October 7, and you already know what happened.

Hanukkah, which ended on Thursday, is an eight-day holiday that celebrates the miracle of the victory of the Jewish rebels, known as the Maccabees, against the powerful Greek army in Judea, and the subsequent miraculous duration of the sacred oil used to celebrate the event in the Holy Temple in Jerusalem, which was only enough for one day but ended up lasting eight.

These days there aren't many opportunities to believe in miracles (I won't even bother to mention the faith in God).

A survey conducted in Gaza this week revealed that 72% of Palestinians support Hamas — specifically, the October 7 attacks — and the formation of "new armed groups" in the West Bank. If we were in a world that values truth, this would shatter the fallacy promoted by the do-gooders of this world who believe that Palestinians are a peaceful people, innocent victims of "colonization."

In other sad news, we learned that three hostages trying to escape were killed by the IDF's "friendly fire," a tragic mistake. The IDF is attempting extremely dangerous missions to free the hostages, but the fighting is fierce and the death toll on "our" side is rising.

The US National Security Advisor Jake Sullivan — whom I detest — is in the region trying to find a path to the "post-war" era and wants to force Israel to accept a Palestinian Authority government (which already governs the West Bank) in the Gaza Strip, something Israel considers unacceptable. Sullivan also wants Israel to reduce the attacks and focus its actions on "capturing" Hamas leaders, as if it were easy.

This is yet another reason for an increase in the death toll on "our" side.

It's been difficult to find reasons for optimism.

Shabbat Shalom.

Suicide Pact

December 17

In its edition this Sunday, *The Sunday Times* published a joint article by British Foreign Secretary David Cameron and German Foreign Minister Annalena Baerbock, urging Israel to adopt a ceasefire.

The article must be important, because it comes with a long comment added in *The Sunday Times* itself and it is also mentioned in today's edition of *The New York Times*.

The proposal is not radical. Right at the beginning, the two ministers of state declare that they do not believe that "calling right now for a general and immediate ceasefire at this moment, hoping that it will somehow become permanent, is the best way forward. It ignores why Israel was forced to defend itself: Hamas barbarically attacked Israel and still fires rockets to kill Israeli citizens every day. Hamas must lay down its arms."

Surprisingly, I agree. Not just with that passage, but with the entire premise of the article.

Every war has a suicidal component. Who, in their right mind, would agree to fight in enemy territory without implicitly accepting a high probability of dying?

However, the situation changes dramatically when you are dealing with an inherently suicidal culture like the Islamic jihadism.

This type of suicidal "warrior," as we all know, only surrenders to death itself.

During World War II, we had the Japanese kamikazes, a clearly suicidal bunch. Only the Hiroshima bomb — actually two bombs, one in Hiroshima and the other in Nagasaki — put an end to their two maniac obsessions: the suicidal and the murderous.

Here, we are once again confronted with the same double rage.

There may be a surrender or two, but the "movement," in its essence, is not concerned with the possibility of dying, much less of killing. As long as there is even one person left infected by this disease, the violence is doomed to continue.

What are we going to do? Keep killing each other until none of them are left? Or, God forbid, no hostages alive? None of us?

With everything we've already said against the Palestinians in this report, it's quite obvious that the faction that motivates and sustains this war differs radically from the local civilians who, regardless of whether they support Hamas, are dying in high numbers. These madmen not only don't care about death — on the contrary, they turn it into a point of honor.

In the "fog of war" — or, as the Israeli military commanders affirm, due to the complexities of war — human sensitivities begin to become dulled, and terrible accidents like the one on Friday, in which IDF soldiers mistook for terrorists three hostages attempting to escape and killed them, become more common.

If we don't intend to drop an atomic bomb on Gaza to put an end to these terrorists' endless suicidal impulses, we'd better start looking for a way out of this situation.

"Finally," concludes the Baerbock/Cameron article, "all those who want to end the suffering need to work together on a solution that delivers long-term security for both peoples. Our Arab partners, in particular, have a crucial role to play in this. They have shown strong humanitarian commitment and have even more political weight to bring to the table. The rise of extremism is a risk to all of us, not just for Israelis and Palestinians."

There is a limit to everything.

And with the Gordian knot currently established in the region, tightened by the prolonged captivity of the hostages with no solution in sight, we need an extra effort to rise up and cut that rope once and for all, no matter which side it's on.

Let me make it very clear that I am not talking solely about Hamas terrorists, who, according to the article written by the two ministers, should be summarily eliminated from the equation, but about the entire Arab world, which certainly can and should do something to change this dire situation.

I may be delusional, but I feel that the time has come.

Diary of a Multifront War

December 18

Beyond the constant sadness of deaths on the battlefield, a battlefield as insane as to include a network of tunnels more spacious than the area above them — the latest news reveals a new tunnel discovered while the others were being flooded by seawater, so wide that a military jeep could easily pass through it — Israel's current intense struggle, unfortunately, includes the so-called "mainstream" media. Or, for some, "legacy, obsolete media."

After publishing in its Sunday edition the insightful article I quoted yesterday, *The Times* of London, disappointingly, decided to include in today's edition another article in which the Archbishop of Westminster deplores the "cruel" murder of two women, a mother and daughter, by an IDF sniper in a church in Gaza. The statement, endorsed by Pope Francis, generated a flood of antisemitic comments saying that the IDF is "out of control," affirming that "now you are seeing the 'true face of Israel,'" and other offenses that, to be honest, I thought it best not to read so I could get out of bed and get on with my day.

There's just one problem: An extensive IDF investigation revealed that the double murder committed in cold blood never happened. Too late, unfortunately, for yet another fatal blow publicly dealt to the reputation of Israel... and of Jews worldwide.

By observing what's happening around me, I've noticed that people are kind of drowning in slogans and becoming so confused that they've started calling Jews "antisemites."

In a "scandalous" appearance at a conservative event in Arizona over the weekend, comedian Roseanne Barr, who has always been known for her outspokenness and provocative behavior, shocked the public with her torrent of insults urging people to vote for Trump and thus "protect us from communists and Stalinists, with special deference to Nazi fascists, and to prevent the Islamic caliphate from taking over all the Christian democracies in the world," or something like that, which, according to her, is already happening.

Radical, to say the least. But there is a world of difference between criticizing that and accusing Roseanne Barr of being antisemitic. The comedian may be crazy, delusional, perhaps she was drunk. But she's also Jewish, and she was clearly deploring the leftist Biden administration and the "woke" abuses committed in recent years against a conservative America that is, ultimately, the America of the vast majority of Americans.

I Aimed at What I Saw...
...And Was Brought Down by What I Didn't See

December 19

A war always has its proverbial "unpredictable" conse-quences — in the case in hand, both unpredictable and shocking, highly disappointing.

Those who follow me know that, until exactly 74 days ago — yes, this war started exactly 74 days ago — the main subject of my essays has been the attack on our children through educa-tion, for example, making them believe that they can change their sex at will and thus eliminating from their lives the most ba-sic certainty that exists, which is biological sex, while convincing those who are mentally fragile to embark on a mutilating journey that leaves them irremediably damaged for the rest of their lives, or telling them that planet Earth is about to end due to a mere one-degree Celsius increase in average temperature, leaving them traumatized and hopeless and lacking the necessary energy to move on with their daily lives, and a whole host of other things I could mention, including that the country they live in, the United States of America, is the most faithful representation of all evil that exists on earth — which is, obviously, the total oppo-site of reality.

Poor children! They are worth all the effort we can dedicate to defending their sanity. However, what I certainly didn't fore-see was that, one fine day, I would wake up and read in *The Free Press* a depressing article showing how they are also being indoc-trinated to hate the Jews.

How is this possible? In a country whose Constitution states that "we hold these truths to be self-evident, that all men are created equal, that they are endowed by their Creator with certain unalienable Rights, that among these are Life, Liberty and the pursuit of Happiness"?

As we all know, all human beings are created equal, including Blacks, Asians, people with all kinds of sexual orientations, men who become women, women who become men. With the (dis)honorable exception of white people, especially white men, and... Jews!

It's too shocking to believe, but it's there, in detail, certified and corroborated by the data included in *The Free Press* article.

None of this would have been exposed, of course, if this damned war wasn't raging in the Middle East, and the wannabe teachers and activists who are poisoning the minds of our children with all the worst possible moral poisons would be free to continue their shameful indoctrination as they've been doing for years.

As my husband Alan would say, take your children out of school, put them in a private school, or educate them yourself at home. Now, with this new addition of the antisemitic element, you can also choose to move to Israel — while Israel still exists.

Joseph McCarthy Was Right

December 20

Like all the "do-gooders" of my generation, I have always considered Joseph McCarthy — who orchestrated a persecution of communists by Congress in the 1950s — an abomination, a horrific, racist criminal.

How awful, this blatant persecution that left Hollywood's best screenwriters out of work — many of them Jewish — simply because they believed that leftist philosophy could improve our lives!

Equality for all! For everyone, regardless of their class or background!

In the several films I've watched throughout my long life on this "delicate" subject, I was at first surprised to find out that, at least in one aspect, McCarthy was right: The screenwriters he went after were leftists, after all.

Of course, at that point, I still believed that the persecution, although justified if we considered the reasoning behind it, was a complete and total horror.

For starters, the motives were basically shameful since in the United States, the land of the free, all people, without distinction, have the right to freedom of speech.

But I have to confess that, over the last few weeks, I've gradually been changing my mind.

Just take a good look at where our tolerance, our desire to respect others — any neighbor, any ideology — has led us, and at the magnitude of the problem we are facing today, here in the US and, in many ways, in every country in the world...

The Marxist doctrine is finally winning, and yet the paradise we were promised has not materialized. And I mean never, in any place or any time. Ask the countless victims of Stalin in the Soviet Union — including Ukraine, where Stalin killed millions during the "great famine" (1930-32)."

Oh, right, you can't ask anybody anything anymore: They are all dead, slaughtered by their own "revolutionary" government, as you well know.

I'm not entirely clear on what exactly ignited Marxist ideals and emboldened Islamic terrorists and their progressive supporters in recent times, especially considering that, in the 1950s, Israel was the ultimate icon of leftist philosophy.

What should now be clear to everyone is that, while they may have once looked like meek lambs, leftists, communists, and the like have always been extremely dangerous wolves in sheep's clothing.

Including... never mind.

Today, with some effort, I could still give them the benefit of the doubt. Perhaps, like I described my own case in the previous note, Karl Marx — and the number of his followers growing over time — shot at the evil they saw and manifested the evil they did not see.

Even so, for me, the time has come to expose the true face of these agents of the devil.

Joseph McCarthy was right, and I didn't know it.

Long live the New McCarthyism. I hope it wipes out this evil from the face of the Earth once and for all. Forever. this time.

Facts, Falsehoods, Opinions

December 21

Everyone is entitled to their opinion, but not to their own facts. — Daniel Patrick Moynihan, US Democratic Senator (1977-2001)

Something pretty weird is happening in the negotiation scenario: Israel, the oppressor party, offered Hamas, the attacked party (so to speak), a seven-day truce — a whole week — so that 40 hostages could be released.

A reasonable proposal, one might say. According to my calculations, 40 hostages are not even close to 30% of the ones still missing, although, of course, we have no way of knowing how many are still alive. On the other hand, given a week, if it had the capacity, Hamas would have plenty of time to regroup, reorganize, intensify its defenses.

Hamas refused.

Of all the possible explanations, I'll stick with just one: Hamas currently has no path to reorganizing and, therefore, a week is worthless to them. The only thing that could motivate them would be a total "surrender" by Israel, that is, for Israel to stop the war for good so they could declare their "victory." Apparently, they are trying to create this "fact."

The UN Security Council has been working for the last four days toward voting on a resolution that would force Israel to accept a ceasefire, which isn't going well because, for that to happen, the United States would have to abstain, at the very least.

It seems that those in favor of the resolution are failing to convince the US, so instead of proceeding to an honest vote, the council is postponing it day after day after day, until the necessary "fact" they want to create becomes possible somehow.

Yesterday, the political scene was busy dealing with a major scandal: The Supreme Court of the State of Colorado ruled, by a 4-3 majority, that Donald Trump cannot appear on the ballot — neither in the primaries in March nor in the presidential election in November.

There is an ongoing initiative to condemn the resolution, which is illegal, as it's practically denying voters the right to vote for their preferred candidate.

It is widely believed that SCOTUS will accept the case and quickly determine that Colorado's decision is... well, as I said, against the law.

Trump has a particular way of bringing to light his enemies' most egregious transgressions — in this case, turning into a fact the assumption that he's being persecuted for political reasons.

According to an article published in *The Free Press*, the only way Democrats believe is valid to "defend" democracy (from Trump) is by... destroying democracy.

The fact is that, despite so many accusations, Trump has not been convicted of anything and is currently the clear favorite — 10 points ahead of Biden — but the Colorado Court decided to create a fact that simply never existed, affirming that Trump created and led an insurrection on January 6, 2021.

Which brings me to my core point here today: In our controversial times, not only do you not have the right to your opinion, but you do have the right to your own facts — exactly the opposite of what common sense dictates and the foundation upon which civilized society rests.

Following the same line of reasoning, in an article published on Tuesday in *The Times* of London, Daniel Finkelstein laments that, of all the comments he received on his previous article — in which he urged the Palestinians to recognize the State of Israel — not a single person on the Palestinian side declared themselves willing to do so, making an agreement essentially impossible. At one point in the article, Finkelstein, who is a reasonably appreciated and widely respected columnist, known as "Lord F" by his readers — not sure that he holds a nobility title, but he's certainly a "noble human," something very out of fashion at the moment — mentions the Golan Heights, adding that "now everyone seems to have fallen silent about it," so I thought I should remind him, in a comment, that he should thank Trump for that.

An inconvenient fact, which was met with an expected cold reaction from the commentators' "community" at *The Times*: zero likes. It's the truth, nevertheless. Among the many things that Trump — the public enemy #1 of half the United States and of the "sensible" people in the rest of the world — did to benefit

Israel, one was moving the American embassy to Jerusalem, and the other, well, sorry, folks… was to recognize Israel's right to the Golan Heights, something that changed everything in the region.

It wasn't by mere chance that "everyone seems to have fallen silent about it." It is simply a historically proven fact, but nobody wants to hear a word about it.

Forgive Them, Lord

December 26

The day after Christmas is as good a time as any to extol the teachings of Jesus Christ, which are, in fact, quintessential Jewish teachings, transformed by the patina of time into "Judeo-Christian" ones.

Yes, although some ignorant activists still insist on reminding us that "the Jews killed Christ" —such as Alexandria Ocasio-Cortez, who in her Christmas message affirmed that "the Palestinians are Jesus Christ" — Glenn Beck, in an excellent article, clarifies how the real story explains that these activists "don't know what they're doing."

We are not here today to condemn anyone, but rather to talk about forgiveness, which, as every psychoanalyst knows, is more useful for the one who forgives than for the one who is forgiven, even if in some cases the benefit is the same.

Imagine the reaction of the IDF soldiers who, by mistake, killed three hostages in Gaza who were trying to escape captivity. Now imagine the reaction of the mothers of those hostages, who, on the verge of achieving freedom, were killed by "friendly fire."

I honestly can't imagine. But the mother of one of these tragic victims — Yotam Haim, the super cute red-haired boy whose photo was everywhere — did something far beyond imagination. When she heard that the troop's morale was low because of the incident, Iris Haim decided to declare, publicly, that she had no anger toward the soldiers involved, "not for a minute."

She felt the pain and the sadness, but understood that the soldiers had done the right thing. And she went even further, inviting them to her home to meet her husband and their three other children, including them in her unbelievable capacity to forgive.

One of the soldiers accepted her invitation.

Now, I don't know if Iris Haim should go down in history as a "Christ incarnate," but I do know that her sensitivity and sense of justice should be an example to the ones among us, myself included, most incapable of putting our own pain aside in the name of a higher ideal.

Love Until the End

December 28

I was here minding my own business, sipping my whisky and finishing the last job of the year before a short and well-deserved break, when a dear friend and fellow Brazilian translator, who lives in Florida, sent me the news that Judy Weinstein, who was believed to have been kidnapped by Hamas, had, in fact, been murdered on October 7.

Only her corpse remains in Hamas's hands.

I had been following this couple — she, 70, not quite sure if she's American or Canadian; he, 73, American — who lived peacefully, flaunting their charm daily at Kibbutz Nir Oz.

Judy Weinstein and Gad Haggai, Z"L.

Gad was declared dead last week (also murdered on October 7) and deserved a page on the White House website, with a special message from Joe Biden.

Apparently, both died after being ambushed by terrorists during their morning walk.

This holiday season I've been thinking a lot about survival, so I couldn't resist the comment: "At least neither of them ended up widowed." But their four children and seven grandchildren were twice orphaned.

After 80, every day is a good day to die, and I myself wouldn't want to face widowhood following the prolific and stimulating life Alan and I lived together for the last 19 years — there's, of course, no rule saying I won't die first, despite the fact that I enjoy excellent health and an admirable disposition, knock on wood. But it is a fact that, in the last decades of life, feeling loved becomes a rather exciting event.

Oh, forget all that. I'm more in the mood for a good glass of champagne on Sunday and just celebrating, and I hope y'all share this simple feeling.

What will be, will be.

Part Two

2024

Sorrowful, but Also Hopeful

January 1

Amid the celebrations and wishes for, let's say, a more joyful new year — if that is something even remotely possible — real life and the war in Israel move forward at their own pace, fueled by sadness and longing for those who are now gone.

It may be difficult, but, at least for me, to support them and be aware is a mandatory duty. Every day. All the time.

So, we begin the new year with a testimony from a couple living in Kibbutz Kfar Aza, which suffered one of the highest numbers of casualties in a single location and is still awaiting the release of six hostages who are residents of the kibbutz. According to the couple in the video, the kibbutz lost 63 people (as of the time of the interview, December 2023).

Their story has moments of deep sadness, but the couple never loses composure, and it ends with a wish, an unbelievable wish given the circumstances: that Israel and Gaza might live side by side in the near future.

The surviving couple and their child, who is less than one year old, came to the United States to try to inform the thousands of young people — who are denying the October 7 attacks and supporting terrorists with chants of violence in the streets of major American cities — of what really happened, and also, unbelievably, to reaffirm that all of this really occurred, as if it made sense for anyone to doubt it.

Incredibly, even today, while I was searching on Google to confirm the death toll — in Kfar Aza alone, because I hadn't written the numbers down while watching the interview — the vast majority of the available links downplayed the real events, mixing information and misinformation. One of these links, believe it or not, states that "despite the sensationalist reports, including the decapitation of babies, the youngest victim was 14 years old." The proof is in the screenshot below.

Despicable, disgusting people. It's a tough call for this couple and others who decide to participate in this "clarifying" mission.

Our duty is to share.

While a massacre of civilians did occur, a few of the most lurid claims, including the baby decapitations, were later found to be false. Evidence provided by Bituah Leumi, Israel's national social security agency, showed that of the 46 civilians that were killed in Kfar Aza, the youngest was 14 years old.

Wikipedia
https://en.wikipedia.org › wiki › Kfar_Aza_massacre

Kfar Aza massacre - Wikipedia

Sobre trechos em destaque · Feedback

Images of the Destruction

January 3

Anti-Israel demonstrations continued throughout the holidays, with participants attempting to cause as much disruption as possible with their shouts and slogans bordering on hysteria, blocking bridges and even the World Trade Center.

The house in which the remains of 12-year-old Liel Hetzron were found, last November.

We have chosen to observe a respectful silence in honor of the victims of October 7, as a protest in favor of the immediate release of all hostages.

In the drip-by-drip notices of death, Ilan Weiss, 71, another resident of Kibbutz Be'eri allegedly taken hostage, was declared dead on Monday, January 1. His wife and daughter, Shira and Noga, who were also kidnapped, were released in November. His brother and sister-in-law, Amir and Mati, aged 69, were killed on October 7.

On the more or less positive side of the news, the year is starting off on the right foot:

• The controversial president of Harvard, Claudine Gay, has just resigned. But don't you rush to the conclusion that it was a reaction against antisemitism or a result of her refusal to criticize Hamas's supporters; in fact, it was due to 45 (no, wait, 50!) accusations of plagiarism in her doctoral thesis... with a special touch: The new (interim) president of Harvard, Alan Garber, is Jewish.

• The IDF has just announced the death, in Beirut, of Hamas's second-in-command, Saleh al-Arouri. They also announced that they will withdraw some troops from Gaza, which is good news. The disheartening part is that they are preparing to fight throughout the whole year of 2024.

This is Day 89, January 3, 2024.

Destruction, but With Utmost Precision

January 4

Don't get me wrong. I'm a peaceful person and I will always defend peace... depending on the circumstances.

The "circumstances" aspect was the central theme of yesterday's editorial in *The Times of Israel*, claiming that October 7 was a watershed moment. Everything that was valid before October 7 is no longer valid today. Everything we defended before October 7, we no longer defend today.

I'm also not a fan of advanced war technologies. I have never felt "exhilarated" while watching a movie or documentary in which some heroic strategy leads to the victory of good over evil, and I seriously hesitate to accept that a dichotomy between good and evil truly exists in this world.

Or at least, I wasn't a fan. I didn't feel exhilarated.

As David Horovitz stated in his excellent editorial, everything changed after October 7, and for me it was no different. But even so, even while supporting Israel unconditionally, I am obviously troubled by the extensive destruction in Gaza, although I don't feel qualified to criticize or even comment on any military — or strategic, for that matter — decision made by the IDF.

I reaffirm my confidence in Israel's leadership, with a slight political doubt here and there, recognizing that this is not the time for any political decision that does not involve the ongoing war — a disposition that, incidentally, Netanyahu has been respecting. Just this week, the Israeli Supreme Court rejected that law which, just a few months ago, radically divided the country in half and filled the streets with enraged protesters, something that might have contributed to the terrorists' conclusion that the ideal moment for the attack had arrived.

And that's exactly how they advanced.

Taking all these elements into consideration, I couldn't help but be impressed by the IDF's surgical precision in Tuesday's attack. It's worth noting that "surgical precision" has long been a euphemism for the reduction of widespread violence in the age of drones — cheap unmanned devices that can do a lot of damage, especially in the hands of unskilled pilots — but let's be honest here: Locating the cunning Hamas commander in Lebanon, in a Beirut suburb, on the third floor of a building, was no small deed. They stopped just short of exclusively blowing up the room where the criminal was hiding...

Okay. okay. No further comments are needed.

As Horovitz explains, it was a risky maneuver. Saleh al-Arouri was the main negotiator for the release of the hostages in Qatar and, as we know, the safety of the hostages is above everything, but, oh, well... Everything changed after the previously unimaginable attack of October 7.

Day 90: January 4.

The End of Israel…
…According to the President of Iran

January 5

Tucker Carlson, of whom I was a huge fan when he was at Fox News, was always against US aid to Ukraine.

His argument was that both countries involved, Ukraine and Russia, were equally corrupt, and America could do better investing our taxpayer dollars in the defense of our own borders and resolving our own internal problems.

At the time, I thought it made some sense, despite my sympathy for Ukraine, which, after all, had been invaded without justification by its more powerful neighbor. But I always thought that the unconditional condemnation of Russia and all Russians was idiotic, going as far as canceling concerts and operas featuring Russian performers — who, as everyone knows, are among the best in the world.

I don't remember ever doing it, but I've always felt tempted to defend the Russian people, who, I believe, are not all exactly represented by the popular image of thugs and traffickers of defenseless women.

Russia is a cultural pillar of civilization, which gave us Dostoevsky, Solzhenitsyn, Nureyev, Maya Plisetskaya, Stravinsky, Tchaikovsky, Wassily Kandinsky — I could spend all day here mentioning the art giants who are native to Russia. Ukraine isn't far behind, especially considering that, well, for a good part of its history, Ukraine *was* Russia.

My maternal grandfather was of Russian descent. Alan's grandparents came from Odessa, Ukraine — which was Russia at the time.

So, today, I learned that Tucker Carlson — whom I stopped listening to when he started with this assumption that the left's "next step" to eliminate Trump's competition could only be "the assassination of the Republican presidential candidate," come on, give me a break — is giving Israel the same anti-aid "treatment."

Let's see how that goes.

I'm not going to burden you with another long list of names featuring prominent Israeli cultural figures, but I feel the obligation to emphasize the differences between the two situations: in Ukraine, a conflict between two nations; in the Middle East, a conflict between barbarism and civilization, plain and simple.

On Wednesday, during the "celebration" of Soleimani's assassination by the US during the Trump administration — may God keep him in hell forever, Soleimani, obviously, not Trump — a terrorist attack in Tehran killed more than 100 people.

The legacy media and the usual protesters didn't waste a second in attributing the attack to Israel, but let's be honest here: I have never heard of a Jewish "terrorist" killing hundreds of innocent people for no reason.

The endless public discussions over the past two days have claimed, on one side, that the perpetrator could only be Israel (and its partners in crime, the United States), while, on "our" side, the argument was that the attack lacked the "trademark" of an Israeli action — namely, the surgical precision that killed al-Arouri in Beirut.

The controversy, with its proverbial antisemitic touch, lasted until last night, when ISIS claimed responsibility for the explosions, all very much in the ISIS style, yes siree. But during the noble event, the Iranian president rushed to declare that the October 7 attacks would end up destroying Israel.

Now take a good look at who we are fighting against: All you need to do is examine the crowd listening to Ebrahim Raisi's provocative speech "praising Hamas," according to *The Times of Israel*. You'll immediately notice that something is missing; there isn't a single woman present.

Of course, my friends. A woman's place is in the kitchen, quiet and illiterate, and dressed in black from head to toe!

Therefore, you barely need my help to differentiate between the two conflicts underway, contrary to Tucker Carlson's "generalization." Just use your own eyes, your own observation skills.

Shabbat Shalom.

Genocide My Ass

January 11

"Noa Argamani, an Israeli citizen, is still in Gaza. She can't testify," says the ad created by the Israeli government to be served in the Netherlands during hearings at the International Court of Justice in The Hague, where Israel is being accused of genocide.

The ad was rejected by all media outlets, in a clear impediment to freedom of speech.

The accusation of genocide is being raised by South Africa, which should obviously be considered a subject matter expert given the tendency toward violence of the dominant group in the country — currently a threat to white residents, officially considered a "conspiracy theory" but, in reality, a reaction to the apartheid years.

Speaking of which, Israel is also being accused of apartheid. But not officially. Not yet.

The official lexicon defines genocide as "a crime committed with the specific intent to destroy, in whole or in part, a national, ethnic, racial or religious group," but the October 7 attack was not even mentioned in the Hague trial underway this Thursday.

It's worth noting that a justified war to defend a country that was attacked is not included in the definition of genocide, nor is it considered prohibited. No country has the obligation to accept its own destruction without uttering a sound, and proof of this is that we also have "official rules" of war, which Israel always strives to obey.

Incidentally, it's worth remembering that the term genocide was created in 1944, *specifically* to define what happened to the Jewish people during World War II.

Today, ironically, it is the Jews who are being accused of genocide and considered the "Nazis" of our time.

The world keeps turning but often doesn't get anywhere. Hopefully, this absurd, one-sided accusation in this so-called "international court" will not become yet another attack on Jewish identity, which, throughout history, for reasons I cannot comprehend, has been under constant threat, even in the world's greatest democracies — of which, by the way, Israel is the best example.

The New Champions of the People

January 12

Last night, while I was gathering material to write about the Houthis, a joint US and UK force, with the alleged support of Australia, Bahrain, Belgium, Canada, Denmark, Germany, Italy, Japan, the Netherlands, New Zealand, South Korea and Singapore — all signatories of a joint statement published on the official White House website —attacked several positions held by the Houthis in Yemen.

One of the articles I had selected, published in *The Times* of London prior to the attack authorized by Prime Minister Rishi Sunak, attempted to explain who the Houthis were, and I wouldn't waste my time mentioning it if it weren't for the discussion the article raised, regarding the photo of a five-year-old Yemeni boy brandishing a machete.

Believe it or not, readers were divided. Some deplored the image — which clearly demonstrates how hatred is inculcated in future terrorists since early childhood — while others defended it with the argument that the knife was simply "part of the traditional attire."

Let's be honest here. Even if that were the case, what kind of terrible example is being set for such young children?

The Houthis, as everyone knows, is another terrorist group — also sponsored by Iran, of course — that has been trying for about two months to interfere (or rather, aggravate) the already super-tense situation in the Middle East by attacking ships in the Red Sea with their cheap drones, causing massive damage to international trade, as 30% of the world's maritime freight uses this route.

That is, it used to. Right now, major global logistics companies like the Danish Maersk have begun to avoid the ancient body of water that, according to biblical tradition, Moses crossed by way of a miracle on his way to the land of Canaan (future Israel), some 5,784 years and five months ago.

Okay. Why should you care?

Don't let yourselves be fooled. The Houthi provocation is already causing a rise in global inflation, affecting my, your, all of our wallets — which have barely recovered from the covid crisis (lowercase, please).

Between you and me, this Houthi audacity is nothing new. The group, based in Yemen, has been waging a "proxy" conflict against the Yemeni government since 2015 — with the national government being supported by Saudi Arabia and the rebels by Iran.

One factor that could eventually favor Israel is the deep-seated hatred between Iran and Saudi Arabia; I would venture to say that few readers are aware of this, and why would they be? Until the problem is felt in our pockets, we apparently had nothing to do with it.

Nevertheless, even before yesterday's military action, the noisy left-wing groups — former limousine socialists, now masked destruction vocalists — had already migrated from their total, unconditional, and musical support for Hamas to... believe it or not, total, unconditional, and musical support for the Houthis, chanting around their new slogan in New York City during their New Year's Eve disturbance: *"Yemen, Yemen, make us proud. Turn another ship around!"*

How could I prove to you that these boisterous leftists, with their antisemitic attitudes, haven't the slightest idea of what they're defending?

I could start with the slogan on their flag: *"God Is Great, Death to America, Death to Israel, Curse on the Jews, Victory to Islam."* That much we could understand, since Israel and the Jews have been the target of these protesters since October 7. They surely prefer terrorism to Judaism... and then they accuse us of defending a genocide (committed by the terrorists in real life), but I don't even need to go that far. The very chanting in New York City is the best argument to demonstrate the ignorance and shallowness of these people; it's not Yemen, the country, that is disturbing the ships in the Red Sea, but the Houthis, who have been official enemies of the Yemeni government for about 20 years.

This whole situation is quite exhausting, I'll give you that. Shabbat Shalom.

100 Days

January 14

On a YouTube video published today you can see the protest in front of the UN marking 100 days of captivity for the hostages in Gaza.

In the 24-hour vigil in Tel Aviv, a single word stood out from all the others, reflecting the sentiment of the 100,000 people present, plus mine, yours, ours.

Bring the hostages back.

NOW
וַיִּשָּׁבַע
الآن
AGORA
JETZT
MAINTENANT
SUBITO
СЕЙЧАС
NÅ
ŞIMDI
NUN
今

100 Days of Brainwashing

January 15

This weekend, in capital cities around the world, hysterical crowds gathered to shout in the streets against the "massacre of Palestinians by Israelis."

Or should it be the other way around?

Ironically, probably without any of these manipulated pawns being aware of it, the trigger for these particular demonstrations was a macabre date, albeit not related to their slogans; a massacre, yes, but not the one they are deploring.

We certainly also had a few demonstrations by Israelis and Jews against the prolonged, illegal, and inhumane captivity of October 7 hostages, but, for some mysterious reason, our pain and our destruction failed miserably to move the masses around the planet.

Even so, there's no erasing the historical truth that this weekend marks 100 days of torture, 100 days of shame, 100 days of antisemitism, 100 days of manipulation of public opinion.

It is true that many died in Gaza, but as victims of a defensive war. Most of the dead, in fact, are Hamas militants, cruelly mixed with poor civilians who are treated as cannon fodder. But not by the Israelis.

The curious thing is that civilians in Gaza are well aware of the situation and don't close ranks with these well-dressed, well-fed, well-groomed, diversity-loving protesters, sheltered in their politically incorrect Western consumerist comfort — which, by the way, would cease to exist if they finally got what they so desperately want.

In stark contrast to the demonstrations in Iran that we mentioned the other day, most of those demonstrating in the West are women. They should all, together with their LGBTQ+ friends and allies, go spend some time in the Arab countries they love so much to find out exactly what and who they're dealing with.

Over the past four years, it has become common practice to finish all righteous and articles well-written by pundits criticizing what's wrong with Western civilization by blaming Donald Trump, so I'll end with him as well, although my writing might not meet the bar set by these talented, paid exponents of media manipulation.

Today marks the start of the presidential campaign with the Iowa primaries. I considered several candidates, but I must confess that, at present, my preference has returned to Donald Trump, on whose shoulders rests the responsibility of being the only personality capable of putting the world back on track despite all the lies published about him and around him — such as, for example, the lie about global warming. Ironically, it's bitterly cold in the United States and the Iowa primaries are taking place in the coldest weather ever recorded for the democratic event in the country's history, -10°F, with a chilling wind on top.

The Loudest Silence in the World

January 17

This Sunday, Hamas did something that, before these nightmarish characters entered our daily lives, we would have thought only existed in horror movies. The terrorist group released an undated video — which, incidentally, I couldn't find online — featuring three hostages, a woman and two men, urging Israel to do something, I don't know exactly what, so that they could be released.

Shortly afterward, Hamas reported that some of the hostages in the video were alive and others were not, and that they would unravel the "mystery" on Monday.

Seriously.

Keeping its promise — a promise whose sole purpose was to spread terror — Hamas released the news that the two men had been killed by IDF bombings.

Their bodies remain "in custody," as is customary with these monsters.

Of course, I didn't believe for a minute that the cause of death, later corroborated by photos of the bloodied bodies, lay with the IDF, something later confirmed by their spokesman. I repeat I was certain that the IDF hadn't killed those hostages, and indeed they didn't.

Even those of you who don't blindly trust the IDF, like I do, must have already realized how the IDF operates: based on facts and on truth. The terrible episode in which three hostages were mistakenly killed while trying to escape is the clearest proof possible: The IDF didn't try for a second to evade responsibility; quite the contrary.

The facts keep piling up, and conversely, the scandal of large numbers of people, government bodies, and celebrities supporting Hamas is growing non-stop.

How dare you?

Hamas doesn't let us forget for a minute that we still have over 130 Israelis in captivity —between the living and the dead — not to mention the deafening silence of the "crème de la crème" of our outstanding society regarding the victims of rape and sexual violence, both on October 7 and in captivity.

Hearing these unresolved facts again and again really hurts, but it's an obligation.

On the very Monday of Hamas's "revelation" about the dead bodies — also Martin Luther King Day — hordes of politically correct barbarians filled the streets of New York. Not even the civil rights icon, poor guy, escaped the wrath of the crowd, who shouted: "MLK, shame on you, you support genocide too."

In front of the Memorial Sloan Kettering Cancer Center, also "accused of genocide" — I failed to understand why — the protesters kept shouting: "Shame! Shame!"

I kind of agree with them. How else could I qualify going out into the streets to defend the brutal acts of terrorism we have been enduring for 103 days?

Shame! Shame!

Happy Birthday, Kfir Bibas

January 18

Yesterday morning, I received an email from a dear friend and reader of my daily column, beginning with the following words: "I continue to think that humanity is seriously ill…"

It wasn't the first, and unfortunately, I don't believe it will be the last.

At the beginning of this series of notes, I speculated whether the war would last 6, 30, or 60 days, compared to other wars Israel has faced throughout its history.

It's Day 104 and I feel stuck, like I'm living through the movie *Groundhog Day* (1993): I write my column in the morning, schedule it for the next day, send it to my readers at 8 or 9 am (depending on the time zone), and receive an email from my friend, which is a comfort to me. Then, I check the news, particularly *The Times of Israel*, choose the story that affects me the most, select a photo, write my column, schedule it for the next day, send it to my readers at 8 or 9 am, and, God willing, tomorrow I'll receive another email from my friend, which is a comfort to me.

For the hostages in captivity there is little to no consolation. There will be no birthday party for little baby Kfir Bibas, who has been living in captivity for 104 days in a dark tunnel and turns one year old today, with no pictures, no balloons and with a lot of rockets… exploding in the distance.

And here I stop and take a deep breath before being able to complete my sentence: Provided he is still alive.

It doesn't seem possible at the moment to predict when this torment will come to an end.

According to the "great victory" negotiated in Qatar, Israel will be allowed to send medications to the hostages who suffer from chronic conditions being held for 100+ days without any treatment. How many will still be alive?

Okay. Let's talk about politics. A few minutes ago (as I explained above, I'm writing this on Wednesday morning to publish on Thursday), in a "burst of heroism," the Biden administration (re)classified the Houthis as a terrorist group.

Let's be very clear: On January 20, 2021, almost exactly three years ago this Thursday, after swearing on the Bible before a crowd, Joe Biden, among a list of executive orders undoing everything good and right that had been done by his predecessor, with a stroke of his pen canceled the "qualification" of the Houthis as a terrorist group.

The result is right there before your very eyes.

It's been like this for the last three years: Biden undid everything Trump had done and is now reversing, after doing a lot of damage, all his misguided decisions, one by one, amidst the largest influx of illegal immigrants into the United States since the country's inception, causing countless problems that have spread far beyond the already strained cities on the southern border and reached major northern cities like Chicago and New York — formerly known as "sanctuary cities."

One curious point is that all the electric vehicles — which the government intends to make mandatory in six years (which will certainly pass in the blink of an eye) — are currently parked because the batteries froze under the very low temperatures, oh, yeah, that's right: When deciding to eliminate gasoline cars, nobody considered the possibility that temperatures would go down instead of up.

Nothing, absolutely nothing that this government intended to do worked in real life. The failure and sheer embarrassment of DEI (Diversity, Equity, and Inclusion) policies (I like to spell it DIE) are just another detail recently exposed amidst a torrent of academic plagiarism, and with each passing day it becomes harder to convince the voters, who will return to the polls in November, of the wisdom of this "leftist revolution" to which we are being subjected against our will, against the most basic logic of the facts.

Hopefully, we will still have a world in November to express our choices through our vote.

The Saddest Birthday in the World

January 18

The world of people who have a heart are mourning in unison the first birthday of Baby Kfir Bibas, known as Gingi, which is the affectionate term in Hebrew for "a person with red hair."

Who are the ones responsible for this dire situation, capable of such cruelty?

Release the hostages. Now.

Gruesome Details

Day 105
January 19

Did you enjoy the photo of the likable 19-year-old IDF corporal, Adir Tahar?

You should know that, in December 2023, his head was listed for sale on the internet for US$10,000.

Right, it seems like these notes are becoming bloodier and more radical by the day. But it's not because of me, my friends; these gruesome details are being revealed sparingly, in homeopathic doses, often by the victims' own families.

The news was published in yesterday's edition of *The Times of Israel*. In an interview with Israeli television, the boy's father recounted that, ten minutes before burying his son — who died after being hit by four grenades launched by Hamas on October 7 — he realized that a crucial part of the body was missing and spent two months searching for the head without much success, scouring videos published by terrorists on social media, where, eventually, he found one showing his son's decapitated corpse.

In December, he recounts, a "miracle" happened: One of the terrorists captured and interrogated by Israel's Shin Bet intelligence service confessed that he had tried to sell Adir's head and revealed its location.

The IDF found it inside a bag in an ice cream shop's freezer, and, weeks later, after it had been properly identified, the head was finally buried alongside the rest of the body.

Sorry to bring this up. Shabbat Shalom.

The Enemy Within

January 22

There is something rotten in the Kingdom of Denmark, and the rot is spreading.

Some hallucinating readers posted comments in a *Times of Israel* article congratulating Israel for being such an evolved democracy that it legally allowed a demonstration in one of the country's largest cities urging Palestinians to victory.

I'm sorry?

Frankly, everything in this life has a limit, and as another *Times* reader pointed out, that limit was exceeded on Saturday.

Don't get me wrong. I'm not condemning my fellow Israelis. Many elements contributed to this moment of profound meaninglessness:

1. Political involvement and antagonism are traditional among Jews, as evidenced by the old joke that "where there are two Jews, there are three political parties."

2. Young people in Israel, as in the rest of the world, tend to lean left, in contrast to the government, which has a certain right-wing tendency.

3. The people are hurt, tired, and frustrated because it seems to them that the government is not giving due attention to the liberation of the hostages, prioritizing the war and the destruction of Gaza instead, which, in my view, is a lie, or at least a serious mistake.

I could add to this list the fact that Israelis, like anyone in any other country — and young people in particular — are being heavily influenced by social media and catchy slogans, leaving little room for reflection on what is true or isn't true, but I prefer to leave that factor out of the so-called "normal and observable" things.

Much has been said about the decline of the "American empire" and the radical reduction of American power in the world, but anyone who agrees with this is failing to use their powers of observation.

The most-used app in the world may originate from China, but most of the nonsense being spread, unfortunately, comes from the United States, where young people are heavily influenced by the overwhelming hegemony of leftism in universities over the last 20-plus years.

The moral confusion these people are exhibiting regarding the reality of life is becoming so high, and so serious, that it can now be described as a deadly disease. Literally, not just the death of common sense, but probably the physical extermination of an entire civilization if we don't take urgent action.

In the case of Israel, the contamination became obvious in the insane demonstration in Haifa last Saturday, in which participants, whether aware of what they were doing or not, shouted encouragement for their own extermination.

Not even Freud could explain it.

The external enemy is easy to detect, and when I refer to the "internal enemy," I am not referring to Israeli citizens who demonstrate against their own country in a war situation, but to the inner enemy of each individual who, under favorable conditions, begins to defend self-extermination as the only possible solution.

****

In other news, rumors seem to be gaining traction that ongoing negotiations to end the war are taking place, with the participation of the US and Arab countries such as Egypt and Qatar. Part of this, I believe, stems from the notion coming from the United States that "only" 20-30% of the terrorists were killed by Israel, falling far short of the expected results.

Look, I don't know if I'm in favor of a Palestinian state adjacent to Israel or not, especially considering a shocking article I read this weekend in the *American Thinker*, which simply states that if we allow a Palestinian state, Israel will eventually be destroyed.

Netanyahu, whom I have always trusted, and who has once again become strongly and openly criticized — including by the editor-in-chief of *The Times of Israel*, a newspaper I mention often — reaffirmed that he will not allow the "two-state" solution that most of our allies are seeking.

However, it is becoming more obvious by the day that some agreement needs to be reached and that this war might not be able to afford waiting for a "victory" to reach its end.

The Answer Is Yes!

January 23

By now you must have realized that I'm extremely worried about the outcome of the war in Israel, and also anxious to know how and when this outcome will come.

So, yesterday morning, I asked Alan what his honest opinion was about the infamous "two-state solution."

"Alan, are you in favor of a Palestinian state?"

"Yes," he replied. "In Africa."

He was being ironic, of course, and he didn't mean, for example, Egypt, whose geographic location in Africa many people ignore. His response was a reference to a story that few people know about the early days of Zionism, when Theodor Herzl, in 1903, attempted to create a Jewish state in Palestine (a place which, it bears repeating, has nothing to do with the current Palestinians) and instead received an offer from the British government to create it in Uganda.

On a more serious note, Alan commented that "a state includes the right to an airport, a navy, and an army," making his true opinion quite clear.

Shortly after that conversation, I came across an interview in Konstantin Kisin's podcast, *Triggernometry*, with the former CIA agent Mike Baker.

At one point, KK asked Baker if he believed that the current world situation was, in some way, due to the Biden administration, and the affable former agent tried to dodge the question while I, in sheer desperation, tried to emulate Congresswoman Elise Stefanik, and, from my stationary bike, started yelling at the TV: "Yes! The answer is YES!"

I think Baker might have listened, because from that point on, the former secret agent dropped the mask and began to paint a perfect picture of the situation, including the Middle East, clarifying several doubts and points.

Baker's final conclusion was both hopeful and surprising.

It was worth every minute.

The UN, Huh? Who Would Have Thought?

Day 113
January 27

Just when we thought that, with its many missteps, the UN had already hit rock bottom and deserved a proper breakup, we saw this Friday that its problems run much, much deeper.

Secretary-General António Guterres, who is Portuguese, declared himself "horrified" by the news that members of UNRWA (United Nations Relief and Works Agency for Palestine Refugees in the Near East) participated in the October 7 attacks — well, um, we know where the Secretary's preferences lie, as well as those of the numerous and diverse UN "committees," each more biased and radical than the other.

One can't go back and rewrite the past, but, in any case, several countries — the United Kingdom, Australia, Italy, Finland, and Canada, led by the United States — decided to put their foot down and hurt the organization where it hurts most: by withdrawing their funding.

Despite the Palestinians' reaction affirming that "the Israelis were threatening and blackmailing the UN," the agency with the unpronounceable and unspellable acronym rushed to dismiss 12 of its employees who were allegedly involved."

"Blackmailing and threatening" are not exactly Israel's *modus operandi*. On the contrary, the country deals with facts and evidence. A high-level Israeli representative had told Axios that "Shin Bet and the Israeli Defense Forces provided information pointing to the *active* participation of UNRWA personnel, as well as the agency's vehicles and facilities, in the October 7 massacre" (emphasis added).

Previously, we had already heard allegations that the Red Cross was sabotaging the delivery of aid and medicine to Israeli hostages. We also know, based on common sense, that without immense support and publicity efforts, a small group of fanatics in Gaza would never be able to mobilize the world's population in favor of murderers — as we have seen happen since the October attacks.

About three years ago, before I restarted writing after a brief "writer's block" period, I had told a friend, who is also a writer, that I was very discouraged by the direction humanity was taking. At that time, I was worried about racist tendencies and the tyranny of gender minorities trying to disrupt our daily lives, with an emphasis on the indoctrination and sexualization of children. Today, I see that these symptoms were just a scab, and what lay beneath was not a simple focus of pus, but an irremediably widespread metastatic cancer.

Well, I'll take back the "irremediably," because if we continue down that path, we will no longer be able to stay alive. But I won't be able to rest until this UN is dismantled and evicted from its beautiful building in the center of New York City.

Shabbat Shalom.

The High Price of Hunger

Day 115
January 29

Today's edition of *The New York Times* features a highly distressing article about the famine in Gaza, reporting that families are selling their possessions to buy flour and that some people are grinding fodder just to have something to eat.

Israel denies responsibility, claiming that not only are there several trucks parked there without access, but also that Hamas frequently "seizes" the supplies being delivered to ensure its militants are fed first.

Even the leftist *New York Times* is exonerating Israel by stating that Hamas and Egypt are also to blame for the situation, given that Egypt sealed its border and, since the beginning of the war, has been preventing any Palestinian refugees from entering the country, in contrast to the policy adopted by other neighboring countries in the event of war over the course of history, always "prioritizing the lives of civilians."

Everyone agrees that the situation for civilians in Gaza is desperate and that an urgent solution is needed, an urgency that is not limited to Israeli actions.

The article also reminds us that we believed humankind had ceased to use hunger as a war tactic, formerly employed even by the Allies in World War II, but the war in Gaza seems to shatter that illusion — although, I repeat, this is not a tactic intentionally adopted by Israel. Perhaps by Hamas, which is the one that profits most from the terrible images that quickly circulate around the world garnering sympathy for the Palestinian "cause," and doesn't care at all about the suffering of its own "constituents."

Look, I'm no expert in the arts of war, and Alan often says that I understand absolutely nothing about the subject, but I'm still capable of devising a plan to end hunger — and the war in Gaza — in five minutes, faster than Donald Trump.

More than half of the buildings in Gaza are destroyed beyond repair, the population is starving, and the hospitals are no longer operational. What else does Hamas need to surrender, release the hostages, and move toward negotiations?

What are they waiting for?

Just as Israel needs to admit that its initial plan to destroy Hamas without leaving a trace is unfeasible, Hamas also needs to admit that its initial plan to eliminate Israel and all Jews has no basis in reality and that it has lost the war. Although, according to sources, *only* 20% of the tunnel network has been destroyed.

No verdict issued by the "International Court of Justice" in The Hague will resolve this.

The only way forward is to put these mortal enemies around a table — which has happened before — or we would no longer have a world to live in.

If Voodoo Could Really Help...

Day 117

January 31

In Brazil, we have a saying affirming that, "If voodoo really helped, the soccer championship in Bahia would end in a tie." An old friend with whom I often exchange ideas about the situation in Israel confessed to me, the other day, her fear that all the hostages are dead, and I partially agreed with her. But if they are all already dead, what's the point of investing time, hope, and effort in negotiations?

Yesterday, I watched an interview on Fox News with the Prime Minister of Qatar, who was present at the negotiations that took place in Paris over the weekend. The negotiator seemed calm and emphasized Qatar's "historic role" in facilitating agreements between enemies in the region.

Over the next few days, all Netanyahu could do was angrily assert that there would be no agreement to release hostages based on the IDF withdrawing from Gaza plus the release of "thousands" of Palestinians.

The argument makes a kind of sense if we consider the prime minister's promise to "eliminate" Hamas — an objective we've already described as unachievable. But... what about the hostages? And the lives of however many of the 130 or so detainees there may be?

While there's life, there's hope, says popular wisdom. Since we cannot be certain that life still exists, neither can we allow ourselves to lack hope; we cannot allow ourselves not to invest in this possibility, even considering the weakest thread of hope for however many lives there may be.

Living in this constant uncertainty has been utterly unbearable, so reversing this situation would certainly represent a morale boost for the country, the soldiers on the front lines, all of us.

While I was grappling with these thoughts, news of a possible agreement — including a six-week truce and the release of all hostages and Palestinian prisoners in the now-proverbial ratio of three to one — arrived, published by *The Washington Post*, as part of the talks held in Paris with the aforementioned Qatari Prime Minister Mohammed bin Abdulrahman Al Thani.

Bibi, I implore you: Do your part and earn your place in the pantheon of history as the next Churchill, even if it means losing the next election.

The times call for heroism, intelligence, and faith — anything but political interests, considering that the lives of many of our compatriots are at stake.

These unfortunate victims have been suffering in unspeakable conditions for the past 117 days.

And What Does Brazil Have to Do With This?

February 2

The battle for an agreement to release the hostages is heating up, and from our hidden neck of the woods there's little we can do except pray.

We can also use this time to try to understand what is happening and why these tensions are exploding in a corner of the world that, without its constant conflicts, would have little or nothing to do with us, so bear with me for a moment:

- The most important thing for those who are fighting against us is religion, in stark contrast to the growing secularism of Western civilization.

- The priority for those who are fighting us is to secure a place in paradise after death, while for us the priority is our life here and now.

- Human life, our highest priority, has little value to those who are fighting against us. What matters for them above all is being faithful to Allah, their God, and to Muhammad, their prophet.

It's as if we are living on two different planets — let's say, we on the planet of reason, they on the planet of illusion.

How can a battle between these two forces be fought, and even more difficult, be won?

An excellent article published yesterday in *The American Thinker* broadened my understanding of the reality behind this conflict and clearly explains why the entire world is being affected by it.

One of the interesting arguments, actually raised in the comments, is that the "holy war" of Islamic militants includes the strategy of flooding the West with Muslims and, once a certain limit is exceeded, the nation in question is then considered part of "Islamic civilization" (an oxymoron, that is, two concepts that cannot coexist in the same sentence). We have seen this strategy gain visible ground at breakneck speed in several countries, including the United States, since October 7.

Another point, and this is where my former fellow Brazilians come in, is the fact that this so-called holy war for absolute control of humankind is fueled by drug trafficking. Check out this excerpt: "Since 1980, Hezbollah sympathizers have been involved in the production and trafficking of cocaine — in Colombia, in the tri-border area between Brazil, Argentina, and Paraguay, and eventually in Venezuela and other parts of South America."

We are aware of this "sympathy" for Islamic terrorism practiced in the tri-border area, but for those who find it difficult to read political analyses and history books, this argument can be seen with greater accuracy and emotion in movies, more specifically in the third installment of the *Equalizer* series (2023), available on Amazon Prime.

For those who would like to go further, I read this week an impressive article published in 2014 that helps us better understand the "clash of civilizations" and the extent to which everything we read and hear is manipulated and has little to do with reality. The author, Matti Friedman, is also a writer for *The Free Press,* a feast of content ready to be enjoyed over the weekend for anyone who is interested.

An understanding heart can be a big comfort. Shabbat Shalom.

Tunnel Vision

Day 121

February 4

The wonderful Douglas Murray is not Jewish. He's a typical English intellectual with a preference for poetry, which can be enjoyed every Sunday in *The Free Press.*

However, since October 7, Douglas has apparently moved to Israel and has begun dedicating himself 24 hours a day to portraying the local situation, interviewing victims and people on the street, and also expressing his profound thoughts about Israel, the conflict with the Palestinians, the course of this world and the humans in it.

This week we listened to a must-watch conversation between Douglas and Michael Oren, a former Israeli ambassador to the US. I nicknamed it "Tunnel Vision," while trying to kill two birds with one stone: the vision of a civilization (another oxymoron) that prioritizes the construction of tunnels for the practice of evil and the "tunnel vision" of people around the world who fail to see the evil they are defending.

The video also includes a list of all that is good in Israel and needs to be preserved.

As an additional note, in this weekend edition of *The Times of Israel* you can check out an interesting analysis written by Lazar Berman explaining why the release of the hostages is the top priority right now and everything else should be left for later.

I have acquired some bragging rights regarding this, as I'm sure you've heard me defending some of these ideas before… to be exact, three days earlier, when I fiercely defended the idea that the top priority at that moment was to free the hostages.

Hostages at the Grammys

Edited version
February 4

A Grammy snapshot five minutes ago: The yellow ribbon applied to the dress bears the inscription "Bring them home."

The woman wearing it, also sporting a Star of David around her neck, is the singer Montana Tucker, whom I've never heard of and who, according to sources, has 14 million followers on TikTok.

From the Series "Sorrow Never Ends"

Day 123
February 6

An article published in *The New York Times* less than five minutes ago confirmed that at least 20% of the hostages still held by the terrorists are dead.

This amounts to 32 out of 136, and we cannot publish their names, as civilized countries usually do, because we still don't know who they are.

Has anyone ever seen a list of names of those killed in Gaza?

That's right. And it's no use claiming that there are thousands of people. Even in the case of small incidents like those in the West Bank, they are not in the habit of emphasizing the human value of each life.

For us, on the contrary, each victim is a stab in the heart; and now, in addition to all this sadness, we still have to deal with the added terror of this intentional lack of information, not to mention the supreme cruelty of keeping corpses in "captivity" as a bargaining chip.

According to *The Times of Israel*, "Hamas is also holding the bodies of fallen IDF soldiers Oron Shaul and Hadar Goldin since 2014, as well as two Israeli civilians, Avera Mengistu and Hisham al-Sayed, who are both thought to be alive after entering the Strip of their own accord in 2014 and 2015 respectively" — something that could have been avoided if they hadn't ventured into the shark's jaws.

How can we envision two neighboring states coexisting in a situation like this?

Meanwhile, negotiations are dragging on, and families have been informed of these new fatalities.

Furthermore, the article says, "the IDF is assessing 'unconfirmed intelligence' that at least 20 additional hostages may have also been killed," bringing the updated count of the living down to 84.

At this rate, by the time an agreement is reached, it may well be that only corpses will be left to be released. I simply can't believe I'm writing this.

My Tuna Sandwich

Day 125
February 8

Alan likes to tell a story about two workers talking during their lunch break. One of them complains that he's forced to eat a tuna sandwich every day, which he hates. The other retorts: "Why don't you ask your wife to make a different sandwich?" To which he replies: "Wife? What wife? I'm not married."

Well, lately, the routine of waking up, grabbing my phone, and spending one hour reading the news has become my "tuna sandwich," which has consequences in every other aspect of my life.

The other day, for example, I yelled at a woman on the phone about a toothpaste purchase. A toothpaste purchase! Alan complained, but I replied that I needed to vent my anger on someone.

So, today, my tuna sandwich of the day was an article in *The Times* of London regarding the fact that Netanyahu had "rejected" Hamas's offer to release the hostages.

It's not just me. The article is truly outrageous.

It begins by explaining that Hamas was demanding a 135-day ceasefire (true), divided into three "batches" of 45 — frankly, I can't stand this habit Hamas has of dividing the terms of its proposals into "easy" installments.

In the first installment, they were planning to release all women and children — including, with a bit of luck, baby Kfir Bibas, who had his first birthday in captivity — in exchange for [number not specified in the article] women and "children" (that is, young adult terrorists) imprisoned in Israel.

The worst part of the article came in the second and third installments, which offered, respectively, to release all the men (2nd) and, shockingly, the corpses (3rd). No mention of how many Palestinians would be exchanged for these hostages, alive and dead — I started to write "Israelis," but there are people of various nationalities among them, including Arabs — but I will tell you this: Hamas's demand was the release of 5,000 prisoners being held in Israel, including 500 sentenced to life in prison.

From there, the article goes on to criticize Netanyahu as the new Loch Ness Monster, for prioritizing "victory" in the war over the liberation of human lives. Okay, if you say so.

You know that in this series of notes our absolute priority, and then some, is the release of the hostages, but accepting such an agreement would simply mean guaranteeing multiple October 7s in the near future. Simply put, almost all the terrorists already eliminated at such high cost would be immediately "replaced."

Do you understand?

For those familiar with the local *modus operandi*, this Hamas's proposal wasn't meant to be accepted, but rather to be bargained for "as much as possible." It may seem repugnant, but from people who sell human beings in installments, we can expect anything. I don't know what got into Netanyahu for him to lose his temper, but it must have been something, and something serious: Playing with the fate of human lives is no joke.

However, we haven't lost hope yet.

At the moment of this writing, the Arab leadership is meeting in Riyadh, Saudi Arabia, trying to find a way, according to *The Times of Israel*, of "leveraging their willingness to take part in the Strip's rehabilitation after the war in addition to *further integrating* Israel into the region, on the condition that Jerusalem agrees to take steps creating an irreversible pathway to an eventual Palestinian state" (emphasis added).

They seem to be living in a fantasy, but, between you and me, I always speculated that a solution to the situation would come from Saudi Arabia.

While awaiting this so-called solution, I vented my anger this morning by selling my shares in an electric car company whose capital is 60% Saudi Arabian. It's worth clarifying that I'm not willing to invest my meager savings in electric cars at all, not to mention that the company has lost 90% of its value in the three years since its IPO.

God bless and goodbye!

In the near future, who knows, I might finally be able to have a delicious cheese sandwich for lunch!

The Corridor of Discord

Day 127
February 10

It may seem redundant to mention the word "discord" in the context of Israel/Palestinians, but the next operation announced by the IDF fits perfectly into that definition.

For Prime Minister Benjamin Netanyahu, the action is essential for the purpose of defeating Hamas, but it became more dangerous because it was "postponed" while international support for Israel steadily declined — well, it's not like it was unanimous before, was it?

Egypt is threatening Israel and warning that an action in Rafah will jeopardize the decades-long peace treaty with Israel. This is, perhaps, primarily due to Egypt's complete unwillingness to open its border to any Palestinian refugees, Rafah being the destination for all northern Palestinians who followed the IDF's evacuation instructions at the beginning of the war.

And that's not even the worst part. Last Friday, White House representatives told the representatives of Arab and Muslim communities in the United States that the government had "acknowledged missteps" in its support for Israel.

The American government, let's face it, is between a rock and a hard place, now that Biden has been practically declared *non compos mentis* according to the final report disclosed by the special counsel appointed by the Department of Justice to investigate the misappropriation of classified documents by the president when he was, well, a regular citizen, after leaving the vice-presidency, with no right to take any documents with him.

Non compos mentis, to put it simply, it's a Latin expression that means "crazy," "senile," or something along those lines, meaning, literally, incapable of participating in a trial in court to answer for his actions.

The media went into a frenzy and the White House descended into chaos. To make matters worse, Biden decided to make an unplanned "address to the nation" on Thursday night, which added insult to injury when the president declared that "Israel overreacted in response to Gaza" and that El-Sisi was the president of Mexico.

How can someone who cannot be held accountable for their actions and has a "poor memory" govern a country like the US in the current global conditions?

The Democrats, who seem to be out of alternatives for the upcoming presidential election, are doing what they can to eliminate the "detrimental" effect of Biden's initial support for Israel, which was much appreciated: After months of demonstrations in the country's major capitals, it is becoming increasingly clear that this support from the president will cost him many votes and, under the current circumstances, every vote counts.

With all of these crises exploding at once, and the increasing public pressure for an agreement — any agreement — to release the hostages, Israel is, more than ever, in a precarious position.

All we can do is pray.

Shabbat Shalom.

Two Argentinians Coming Back Home

Day 129

February 12

We started the week with some good news: At least two of the 130 hostages still held captive in Gaza have been confirmed alive.

In a "daring" rescue operation, the IDF this morning released two hostages who were found in an apartment in Rafah, on the second floor of a regular building.

Fernando Marman, 61, and Louis Har, 70, both kidnapped from Kibbutz Nir Yitzhak and holding dual nationality, are malnourished, but in good health.

This is only the second successful hostage rescue attempt — the first, back in October, freed the female soldier Ori Megidish, proof of the high complexity involved in this type of operation. (We are still mourning the three hostages mistakenly killed by the IDF.)

Beyond the battlefronts, the diplomatic war continues.

While announcing the news this morning, IDF spokesman Daniel Hagari stated the following: "Even this morning, we haven't forgotten for a second that 135 hostages are still being held captive in Gaza."

Neither did we.

Rafah, an area quite close to the kibbutz where the freed hostages were held, has not yet been the target of an Israeli military operation. The situation has been intensely debated, with the US "demanding" that, before anything else, Israel guarantees the safety of civilians.

According to government sources, this is the last region to be "cleared." The cleanup continues in other locations. Two days ago, the IDF exposed a Hamas sophisticated data center located under the UNRWA headquarters in Gaza City. UNRWA, as we all know, is the UN humanitarian organization with a dual personality: on the one hand, it helps Palestinians in need, on the other hand, it funds and helps Hamas terrorists, including several who participated in the October 7 attacks.

According to the IDF, the discovery of the data center while UNRWA is undergoing "intense international scrutiny" for its support of Hamas is "pure coincidence."

Damned If You Do, Damned If You Don't

Day 130
February 13

Yesterday afternoon, at the White House, Joe Biden and the King of Jordan, Abdullah II, gave a joint press conference. His Majesty was the first Arab leader to visit the White House since October 7.

Jordan, it's worth remembering, is an important player in the region. According to *The Times of Israel*, "about 50-60% of the country's population are descendants of Palestinians." I could say it better: 50-60% of Palestinians (probably more) are descendants of Jordanians, and although today there's no denying that the Palestinians are a separate people, in 1948 they were all Jordanians. If their situation as "war refugees" had not been exploited *ad absurdum* at the time, they would be living happily and healthily today... in Jordan, a beautiful country.

Oh, well. There's no point in trying to rewrite history. Today's Palestinians, numbering in the millions, could hardly be called "refugees," although some camps qualified as such still persist after almost 76 years, probably to justify the billions in international aid.

Jordan and Israel maintain diplomatic relations and reciprocal embassies; perhaps for this very reason, and due to multiple international interests, King Abdullah was emphatic in yesterday's interview when demanding a two-state solution, with Israelis and Palestinians living side by side. Queen Rania has already expressed herself publicly with antisemitic undertones, but at least yesterday we didn't have to listen to the usual litany, "from the river to the sea."

The "river," which is the Jordan River, originates in Lebanon, marks the western border of Israel, and owes its name to Jordan — or perhaps it's the other way around, I'm not sure. In English, or "international" language, the country and the river have exactly the same name: Jordan.

But I digress. Would I be lacking inspiration?

Yesterday, Biden was having a good day: He didn't call the king "president," nor Jordan "Saudi Arabia," but more than four days after the publication of the report affirming that he had memory problems, the media still hasn't managed to change the subject.

What I found surprising is that today we had a rare press conference from the presidency in the morning, and everyone expected that the Biden situation would be addressed.

It was. But not in the way you would think. Despite all the media frenzy and Vice President Kamala Harris's statement that she was "ready" to assume the presidency if necessary — she may be ready for the US, but the US certainly isn't ready for her — the White House's reaction was an emphatic refusal to submit Biden to a memory test.

I don't understand a lot of things, but I understand this even less. Let's say, not for the country's sake, but for the elderly man himself, the first thing they should do would be to subject Biden to this test... unless they're lying.

I know what I'm talking about. My mother died of Alzheimer's after 15 long years battling this terrible disease, and today, although there is no cure, there are some medications that can help. If he had cancer, would Biden refuse to have an MRI? Or to receive the relatively encouraging new treatments?

I don't think so.

Observing Biden in his comings and goings, even I — a layperson and an ignoramus — can notice many signs of this illness, including his stiffness and unsteady gait when walking.

Moreover, the refusal to accept forgetfulness is also a common symptom. The would-be patient has good days and bad days and goes down a path between the first signs and total unconsciousness that has various stages. It all starts by writing everything down as a "simple reminder." My mother kept a calendar on the wall in the hallway, which became increasingly scribbled on.

The end is inevitable. Biden should at least protect himself, since protecting the country he presides over is obviously not a priority.

Human, Simply Human

Day 131
February 14

Some things seem as impossible as changing sex, but Mosab Hassan Yousef — from Ramallah, son of Hassan Yousef, one of the founders of Hamas — after his teenage and young adult years devoted to the "cause," switched sides and became an informant for the enemy, that is, for the Israeli government.

It's not a unique case in history. An even more notorious former terrorist is Maajid Nawaz, a British activist and author of the autobiography *Radical: My Journey Out of Islamic Extremism*, available on Amazon.

But the facts we learned in Yousef's interview with Douglas Murray are nonpareil — shocking, to say the least.

Repeatedly, throughout the video, I found myself asking: "But is he talking about humans?"

The transformation typically began when Yousef, fresh out of adolescence and imprisoned in Israel for buying weapons with the intention of committing terrorist acts — according to him, being in prison fortunately prevented him from committing his first terror attack and all those that might have followed — witnessed the mistreatment, torture, and murders committed by Hamas within the prison against other imprisoned Hamas members, in an attempt to uncover a traitor who was allegedly passing secrets to the Israelis. Yousef confesses to having been afraid that, should Hamas come to power, it would treat all the Palestinians in the same way.

It's surprising that Yousef, instead of feeling cornered, reacted by switching sides, but it doesn't surprise me that, beneath the cruelty with which he was raised, a true human being emerged. Only Freud can explain it.

Yousef, who spoke out again on October 7 after ten years of silence, is quite active on the internet, and his videos can be watched online.

Hospitals (Encore)

Day 133
February 16

Yesterday afternoon, the IDF carried out an operation at Nasser Hospital in Khan Younis, southern Gaza, based on intelligence indicating that some hostage corpses might be hidden in the medical center.

According to *The Times of Israel*, dozens of terror suspects have been captured, including "a Hamas ambulance driver who participated in the October 7 onslaught."

I don't know if the body of Yair Yaakov, 59, also declared dead yesterday by Kibbutz Nir Oz — to be clear, the accurate information is that Yaakov died on October 7 and, although counted as such, was never alive in captivity — was among those being sought.

That's the situation we find ourselves in: Every day the news transfers more people from the "column" of kidnapped hostages to the "column" of corpses held by Hamas. Today, the question of the day is as follows: Why this Hamas fixation on underground hospitals and medical facilities, including, as we now see, ambulances? Did they imagine that public opinion regarding Israel's "attacks" on hospitals would neutralize the horror people would feel regarding their murderous activities?

But what am I saying? People (in general) have never, since October 7, expressed their horror regarding the murderous rage of the terrorist group; quite the opposite. An article published yesterday in *The Times* of London reports that antisemitism in the United Kingdom has increased by 400% during this period.

Let me check if I understand this: More than 1,200 citizens of a country belonging to a specific ethnic group are massacred with extreme cruelty, and instead of revolting and rising up to defend the victims, is the world defending the perpetrators?

If this whole situation seemed improbable 133 days ago, today it seems even more so, but the trend continues. It's as if the moral standards of humanity as a whole have been turned upside down.

Honestly, I'm not prepared to live in a world like this, and the situation isn't getting any better.

Currently, the battered humankind has a new chance to redeem itself. After South Africa attempted to accuse the Israelis of genocide in Gaza, nine families of victims have filed a criminal complaint with the same International Court of Justice against the genocide perpetrated by Hamas in Israel on October 7.

Let's where this goes. Shabbat Shalom.

Let's Talk About Flowers

Day 134
February 17

Vered Libstein, organizer of the annual wildflowers' festival Darom Adom ("Red South"), which she founded with her husband 19 years ago, lived in Kfar Aza, one of the kibbutzim on the Gaza border most affected on October 7. Vered lost her husband,

Ofir Libstein, her 19-year-old son, Nitzan, her mother, Bilha Epstein, and her niece, Netta Epstein, in the terrorist attack.

The war in Gaza continues, but the flowers this year are not only blooming but, according to *The Times of Israel*, exploding with full force.

"Life is stronger than everything," said Vered. Nature doesn't care about human suffering and continues unabated, imposing, unchallenged. On the other hand, and perhaps for that very reason, it is one of the few bastions of mental health that remain to us in an increasingly radicalized world.

I could write yet another of the countless obituaries for Alexei Navalny, the heroic Russian dissident who died yesterday in a prison near the North Pole. The "cause" of death was not disclosed, except that the activist suffered a "collapse" after going for a walk — and we all know how Putin's government operates. The prison refused to release Alexei's body to his mother and lawyer, I wonder why. Bari Weiss, in his honor, wrote and repeated in no uncertain terms in *The Free Press* that the activist was murdered, despite the fact that we have no concrete proof yet.

But this well-deserved obituary is not in my agenda today, the first day of the Presidents' Day long weekend, and my day of choice to embark on my own wildflower journey in 2024.

This is my fourth year growing wildflowers, an experiment I started in another February during Covid, trying to plant poppies, which didn't go very well. Since then, I've learned a lot, both in the garden and in life itself.

This year, I'm trying out several new things, including the daisies I sowed in the fall; we'll see how that works. Better safe than sorry, so I also sowed the usual seeds on Wednesday, along with the annual pruning of the roses, and today I'm going to spread vitamins all over the garden and, for the first time, also include the wildflower "meadow." I bought a new hose and installed it on the deck to have access from above and thus cover the meadow more extensively.

Vered Libstein's grief far surpasses any loss or pain I have ever experienced, particularly because it makes zero sense and goes against the order of nature, but I can understand very well the kind of comfort she finds among her newly bloomed flowers, because I feel it too.

May this approaching spring bring us solace for the difficulties of this life.

Speaking of which, the name of the kibbutz Or HaNer, where the flower festival is being celebrated, means "candlelight." At least I'm using this war to brush up my Hebrew.

Have a nice weekend.

Lula, Who Would Have Thought, Ended Up in The Times of Israel

Day 136
February 19

I'm sure Israel was just waiting for a statement by President Lula of Brazil to understand that things were looking bad for the country, and the wait is now over.

As usual, thanks to the brilliance of his intellect and his impeccable reputation as an internationally renowned politician, Lula exceeded expectations and ended up in *The Times of Israel* with the insightful conclusion that "Israel's response in Gaza is comparable to Hitler's actions against the Jews."

It would be ridiculous if it weren't offensive. Does this mean that Israel, the homeland granted to the Jews as a result of

Hitler's Holocaust and the last bastion of defense for Jews world-wide, is now the "new Hitler"?

Let's face it: God and Hitler have been used too liberally by the ignorant masses who, every day, reveal themselves to be even more ignorant, radical, and absurd.

The only reason I'm not ashamed of being Brazilian is that, not for a single minute of my long life, have I allowed anyone to even imagine that there might be a spark of approval for Lula on my part, however small.

I always considered him a corrupt and ignorant politician with absolutely no historical sense, a fact that has just been confirmed for the umpteenth time, only this time it affected me personally. I know several members of the Jewish community in Brazil, which includes many voters of the PT Party, and I know several of them personally.

I am and always will be grateful to Brazil for the opportunity to grow up in a country where, at least, the fact that I'm Jewish never caused anyone any discomfort. I may have faced all sorts of difficulties in life, including the traumatic fact that, in Brazil, no matter your ability or the intensity of your efforts, you always end up hitting a wall one way or another. Even after ten-plus years living in the "first world," I still expect my endeavors will fail every time the sun comes up... but antisemitism? Never!

Sorry for the rant. Between you and me, we could have been spared Lula's "new low." For that and other myriad reasons, I'm now so proud of being an American.

An Ultimatum

Day 137
February 20

It seems that, after three prime ministers in quick succession and several missteps — including the mismanagement and scandals during Covid — the UK is about to change the ruling party back to Labour.

For much of my life, the Labour Party has been considered the "good" side, with Tony Blair and other prominent figures, but in recent years the party's reputation has plummeted, partly due to the explicit antisemitism of Jeremy Corbyn, who was eventually ousted and, I guess, is not missed.

The issue is that the party now has a new leader, Keir Starmer, described as lacking charisma. But I found him quite attractive in one of the few positive profiles I've read in *The Times* of London in recent years, published last Saturday.

Let's face it: Although it may not seem like it, the world is eager for a new generation of calmer, more technical leaders because, as we know, hell is full of strong and controversial personalities. Overflowing.

Over the weekend, as part of his campaign, Starmer — whose wife is Jewish — appeared to be hardening his stance on Israel by demanding an immediate ceasefire. However, upon closer examination of the proposal, one can see that the condition for this would actually be the release of the hostages. Unconditionally.

The truth is that, despite Netanyahu's continued rhetoric demanding victory in Gaza, the Israeli government itself — which, by the way, has just declared our beloved Lula *persona non grata* — is leaning in the same direction as the UK and the US and does not consider the next attack on Rafah a fait accompli. But of course, this concession cannot happen without certain conditions.

Lo and behold, the conditions came yesterday, in the form of an ultimatum: If Hamas does not return all the hostages by the beginning of Ramadan, which this year will fall on March 10, the feared attack to destroy the last remnants of the terrorist group's power will be launched.

Benny Gantz, a minister without portfolio and a member of the war cabinet, said the following last Sunday: "To those who say that the price [of an offensive] is too high, I say this very clearly: Hamas has a choice — they can surrender, release the hostages, and the citizens of Gaza will be able to celebrate the holy holiday of Ramadan."

That's it. The offer is on the table.

Our nightmare could end in less than two weeks — not exactly the kind of proposal one would expect from a country accused of committing genocide.

Life Goes On

Day 138
February 21

Everybody knows that the image of the world we get from the news is only partially a view of reality. In the case of this war Israel vs. Hamas, for example, I had the impression that, while the army is in action in Gaza, life has completely stopped in Israel.

Today, watching a mandatory interview with Natan Sharansky — a live event of *The Free Press* in Israel — we realize that it's not quite like that. The people in the audience, in the packed auditorium in Tel Aviv, appear smiling and genuinely enjoying the conversation between Bari Weiss and this historical figure. At one point, I even thought I had seen, without actually believing my lying eyes, Jeff Bezos there watching, wearing a kippah.

Chances are it was just someone who looked like him, but then I did some research and found out that, around the same time, Bezos was actually in Israel, negotiating a massive expansion of Amazon's facilities in the country, even though he is no longer the company's CEO.

This is yet another sign that life in Israel hasn't stopped; quite the opposite, in fact.

Sharansky is a sort of living history figure who has been in the spotlight in recent days due to his identification with Alexei Navalny, the Russian dissident who died in prison over the weekend. Sharansky was also a prisoner in the Gulag for nine years before managing to emigrate to Israel, and exchanged correspondence with Navalny, according to exclusive reports published by *The Free Press.*

Once in Israel, Sharansky became a politician and participated in several government cabinets. His work includes taking part in the peace negotiations in Oslo, Norway, in 1993.

In addition to being extremely interesting, the video is also highly informative and provides an unmissable historical perspective from the viewpoint of someone who lived through history, not simply read about it on social media.

The biggest and most surprising highlight, in my opinion, was Sharansky's optimism, which allowed us, amidst all the sadness of this war, to experience some moments of genuine pleasure.

It's worth every minute.

Corpses

Day 145
February 28

In an article published today in the *New York Post*, the widow of Alexei Navalny, the Russian dissident who died last week in Siberia, declared that the activist's body "suffered abuse" in prison before being returned to his mother for the funeral.

The article mentions that Alexei was murdered, but puts the term in quotation marks because, in fact, this has not been confirmed... although, of course, it is more than confirmed: after several poisoning attempts and years of torture in the Gulag, it certainly wasn't a natural death, right?

Navalny was only 47 years old.

Woe is the civilization (or lack thereof) that keeps itself busy with kidnapping, torturing, and abusing corpses, and I'm sure you know what (or who) I'm talking about.

In the Israel-Gaza conflict, things are a bit confusing at the moment, after the decidedly senile and super-duper statesman Joe Biden spilled the beans saying that an agreement had been reached and several hostages (alive or dead, who knows at this point) would be released before the weekend.

That was yesterday, Tuesday (today is still Wednesday, if I'm not mistaken).

There was a general outcry from both sides, because, obviously, the terms were still being negotiated and, as you know, secrecy is the soul of this (negotiation) business.

Biden has in fact "queered the deal"... Oops, I just got informed by Google's AI that this idiom is now considered "offensive" because queers (literally, "weirdos") are now sacred, so I couldn't get Gemini, ex-Bard (the low quality remains the same, but the name…) to accept it. In good Portuguese we would say "entrou areia" (the sand got in), and you know very well where the sand gets in, so I hope the sand doesn't mind being abused this way.

By now, you must be thinking that I'm so desperate with this war and the state of this world that I've given up on my report, but that's not the case at all.

The thing is, Alan had an accident. He was missing *caipirinhas*, the typical Brazilian drink and the only thing he really appreciated in Brazil, in addition to the word "cachaciero,"[7] the only one he could learn in Portuguese.

So, he bought vodka and I made some caipiroskas — a milder version of the drink in which the cachaça is replaced by vodka. They were so delicious that he downed two and, well, you know how that sweet, cold drink affects the body… Anyway, he tripped on the bed and fell backward, hitting his head on the floor.

He was lucky, and to this day I'm thanking God because he didn't have a concussion or fracture his hip; I'm not even sure how that miracle happened. Alan was a gymnast in his teens, so he has some automatic tricks for falling without getting hurt and I have no idea how they work. The bottom line is that he only sprained his ankle, but now he can't walk, and I had to get a wheelchair because, to complicate matters, he's undergoing treatment for another health issue and needs to go to the clinic daily.

With this, not only did I have to give up the luxury of not driving, but I also had to learn to "drive" a wheelchair overnight…

As the French saying goes, this too shall pass. In the meantime, this writer here had to take an unpaid leave of absence be-

---

[7] Cachaceiro: a person who drinks "cachaça," a strong alcoholic beverage made from sugarcane.

cause things are tough, my friends — but don't you worry. I can guarantee my 80-year-old husband is full of energy and bossing me around as always.

See ya later.

What's in a Name?

Day 149
March 3

There is a literary debate about the title of this note: was it written by Shakespeare or by James Joyce? It is certain that the phrase appears in *Ulysses*, but I honestly don't remember whether it's an original line or a quotation. If I'm not mistaken, Joyce never clarified the issue.

But what cannot be disputed (although many people actually dispute it) is that, with each passing day, Hamas seems capable of falling even deeper into the pit of human cruelty, which, for the terrorist group, seems to have no limits.

The latest "refinement" of this terrorist torture technique is refusing to provide Israel with a list of the hostages who are still alive. The latest negotiations have been stalled for... I've lost count, and this weekend the obstacle is the one I mentioned. Unimaginable.

The low number of hostages whose release is being offered is far less than the remaining number of people theoretically held captive in Gaza (130, with 31 reportedly already dead, according to this Sunday's edition of *The Times of Israel*. If "knowledge is power," then keeping us in a state of not knowing is an even greater power in the hands of our enemies.

I don't know what else to say or write about these animals. I'm at rock bottom.

Those who hate Israel like to compare this "low" number to the 300 million — oops, 300 thousand, 30 thousand, and shrinking, who died in Gaza. But they carefully omit the difference between those killed in a war and those killed in a cowardly terrorist attack — 30, 130, 30 thousand, it doesn't matter.

For the relatives who are waiting — and in terms of Israel and Jews, as you know, we are all part of the same family — each name carries an entire world within it.

I don't know about you, but I have reached my limit for quite some time now. Now imagine the unfortunate families of these remaining hostages, kept in constant uncertainty for 149 days.

Give those monsters what they deserve, Bibi!

I Don't Know, I Don't Want to Know, and I Loathe Those Who Do

Day 150
March 4

The vice president of the United States is "toughening her stance" regarding a ceasefire agreement, but it's proving difficult.

In an interview published this morning, a Hamas spokesperson stated that the terrorist group "**doesn't know which hostages are alive and therefore cannot provide a list to Israel**" (emphasis added).

I didn't see it, I know nothing about it, nobody told me, I haven't the slightest idea... Hostages? Which hostages? Israel? What do you mean by "Israel"? I've never heard of it.

The article about it in *The Times of Israel* only has the headline, I've never seen anything like it. It seems like we're living in an era in which things we have never seen abound, so let's stop here.

In other news, which pales in comparison to its importance and lack of meaning, the United States Supreme Court just issued a unanimous opinion, 9-0, preventing leftist states from barring Trump from appearing on the ballot — something we already know is illegal.

Do you understand?

Illegal.

Undemocratic.

Unanimous.

Including justices from both the "left" and the "right."

Obviously, this Supreme Court ruling means that not only Colorado — which litigated the case in plenary session — but also all other 49 states are prevented from undertaking this shameless political persecution.

It may be, perhaps, I don't know, that the age of insanity is easing. To lighten the mood a bit, I can affirm that it seems the first domino has already fallen...

Tomorrow is "Super Tuesday." The expected result is that Donald Trump will be confirmed as the Republican candidate and will, finally, be able to position himself at the starting line for the presidency of the United States.

In yet other news, it seems that a "smoking gun" is now showing that the coronavirus did, in fact, come from the laboratory in Wuhan.

All of this is making history, and you have the dubious privilege of witnessing live this endless collection of blunders.

Have a great week!

Soldiers in White Gloves

Day 152
March 6

Today, in the USA, we are all used to seeing — and verifying — that there is a "double standard" when justice is concerned.

The most obvious sign is the difference in how the now-confirmed 2024 presidential candidates are treated: Joe Biden is the perfect, lucid, and immaculate current president; and his challenger, Donald Trump, is being tried for 91 crimes and has already been ordered to pay a $350 million fine for business dealings conducted regularly in the state of New York.

For this reason, I found myself courting my worst instincts while reading, in today's edition of *The Times* of London, about a "complaint" posted by the investigative website Bellingcat that Israeli soldiers were caught "humiliating blindfolded Palestinian prisoners."

What we see in the photo are some detainees sitting on the ground, with no soldiers present and a person holding a badge that says "Hamas Hunting Club" and "Good Hunting" — an obvious attempt at humor amidst the misery of war.

There is no "Hamas Hunting Club" — apparently inspired by a movie whose name I've forgotten. But the do-gooders, trying hard to destroy all goodness that exists in this world, swooped down on the "investigation" like vultures on carrion, condemning the most ethical armed forces in the world for not requiring that their soldiers wear white gloves and be very cautious not to offend anyone on the front lines.

You know how that goes: Israel, the IDF, and all Jews are judged based on impossible ethical demands, given human nature. But the sacrosanct UN took FIVE MONTHS to come up yesterday with a pathetic document stating that there is a "reason-able" basis to assume that Hamas committed sexual violence on October 7... as if there weren't dozens of videos, oftentimes recorded by the perpetrators themselves, and irrefutable post-mortem evidence of the unspeakable horrors suffered by Israeli victims.

"Double standard" is a euphemism. I hate these people.

International Women's Day

Day 153
March 7

I've always hated this whole "International Women's Day" business without really knowing why. I think it's because I've never seen myself as belonging to a minority, and the very notion that women are a minority — after all, we're 50% of humanity — is as ridiculous as "not knowing what a woman is."

Time has proven me right. All the fuss surrounding women's rights and women's equality has resulted in a situation where, for example, men dressed as women are winning all women's sports competitions and causing serious physical injuries to female play-ers in team sports, but nobody is allowed to say anything for fear of being canceled or some other nonsense regarding "rights."

But under no circumstances has Women's Day proven to be as ridiculous, racist, violent, and prejudiced as in the case of the Israeli women who were kidnapped, tortured, and raped, with-out their suffering being acknowledged by the United Nations or by any of these dangerous ideological groups.

It was no coincidence that Florida, last week, declared these DEI policies and the money spent to support them illegal. Imme-diately afterward, "DEI departments" — veritable nests of leeches — were dismantled, and the parasites who comprised them were fired.

I sincerely hope this is the start of a trend.

As for the Women of Jerusalem: While justice is not served, you can check the emotional and depressing blog post from *The Times of Israel* that names one by one the victims who are still in Hamas's hands — nobody knows where, with no date set for their release, and subjected to God knows what abuses — while none of the morally superior "defenders of rights" in this world give a flying fuck about it.

The Unbearable Lightness of Antisemitism

Day 159
March 13

The old (and now useless) joke about "a broken clock being right twice a day" applies perfectly to President Biden (God willing, soon to be former president).

At the start of the war, I wasted my time expressing gratitude toward Biden regarding his steady support for Israel, a support that seems to be rapidly fading due to pressure from his "peers," all of whom are antisemitic — in principle and practice.

After a "fiery" State of the Union address, fueled by the kind of prescription drugs we all wish we could take someday, Biden plunged back into his deep pit of confusion and dementia. One of the symptoms, as highlighted by the editor of *The Times of Israel* David Horovitz today, would be the president's allegation that Netanyahu "is hurting Israel more than helping Israel" and his declaration, in the same interview, that he "will never leave Israel," but "nonetheless also set out a 'red line' regarding the looming IDF operation in Rafah." (I omitted the part in which Horovitz calls Biden a "Zionist.")

Horovitz recalls, in his mandatory editorial, that only four Hamas battalions remain to be defeated before the war ends.

However, the leitmotif of his column is not the senile American president, nor even less Netanyahu's faux pas (*The Times* editor is not "very appreciative" of the prime minister), but rather the stupidity, ignorance, and ineptitude of the so-called "evolved" Jews, whom I recognize as self-hating Jews — idiots who adopt the language of our enemies just to "stay in the spotlight." In this case, a literal spotlight, since it refers to the director of the Oscar-winning British film about the Holocaust, *The Zone of Interest*. The privileged director Jonathan Glazer used his increasingly less relevant time — as watching the Oscars is completely "out" — to condemn the "occupation" of Gaza by Israel, an occupation which — as I have explained dozens of times — is nonexistent.

Horovitz's own column demonstrates that the gravity of the moment requires us to set aside all our disagreements and stand united, under Netanyahu's leadership, to reach the end of this tragic journey that is the current war against Hamas.

Regardless of your opinion of the prime minister— Horovitz's against him, mine in favor — he's the one at the helm, and any division at this moment would be fatal for us.

Kamala Harris vs. Israel

Day 171
March 25

Kamala Harris, our incompetent Vice President, recently assumed her new persona as a "stateswoman" and decided to... declare war on Israel.

Let's face it, in the three years and three months since she took office, not a single day has passed without the media from "both sides of the political spectrum" turning the vice president into a joke.

Until last Sunday, her incompetence was one of the few things that we Americans unanimously agreed upon, with the possible exception of left-wing radicals — for whom the fact that she is a "woman" and a "person of color" automatically puts her on a pedestal and makes her untouchable.

Until last Sunday, all the tasks assigned to Kamala Harris were a testament to her — shall we say — lack of talent. Then yesterday, in an interview with CBS, the vice president displayed her revamped persona for the first time.

I don't know how that happened, but the truth is that the vice president seemed focused and composed. She didn't mince words and remained carefully away from her proverbial "word salad" and uncontrolled giggles.

However... in the long-awaited debut of her "political redemption" — considering that her boss seems to be accelerating his journey toward senescence — Kamala decided to declare war on the biggest and most traditional US ally: Israel.

It seems crazy that a vice president would take such a strong stance against an ally. The result, coupled with the UN approval, a few minutes ago, of the resolution demanding an immediate ceasefire, was that Netanyahu ended up canceling the Israeli delegation's trip to Washington to discuss precisely the issues surrounding the future of the war and the Rafah operation — exactly the subject of Kamala's interview.

That was all we needed in a moment such as this: to have our most important and practically only ally turning against us and joining forces with the global antisemitic movement.

I don't know in what world Kamala Harris lives, but to me, although the format has changed, her brain still seems to be disconnected from the rest of her body... and from the rest of the world.

In an excellent article published this morning in the *American Thinker*, the lawyer and editor Andrea Widburg wrote the following: "So remember, if you vote for anyone but Trump (and this is true whether you like Trump or not), you are voting to keep in office a man who is literally siding with the Nazis of 2024."

Unfortunately, this is totally true.

Speaking of which, I don't think that the above-mentioned UN resolution is completely awful, considering it demands the release of all hostages as well. To be confirmed.

"The Devil Possessed Me"

Day 176
March 30

It is true: I no longer have the energy or the will to continue describing the atrocities of October 7 and beyond.

But our enemies — and the enemies of the goodness that still exists in humanity — continue to debate whether or not "there was sexual violence" during the terrorist attack and then later, toward the hostages in captivity.

Just now, while searching on Google, I watched the first two minutes of a video on The Intercept — the website formerly created by Glenn Greenwald to be "liberal and fair" — claiming that there was a lack of "convincing" evidence for the "controversial" article published in December by *The New York Times* about, well, sexual violence on October 7.

A discussion on this subject shouldn't even exist. Honestly, it should be listed among the worst horrors in human history, period. But people insist, to the point that now the victims of violence feel obligated to recount, firsthand, what happened to them — like Amit Soussana, who this week had the questionable honor of being "the first former hostage to publicly reveal that she was a victim of sexual violence while in captivity in Gaza." With all the details.

As the media's thirst for horror stories seems to never subside, *The Times of Israel* decided to publish a clip in which a terrorist captured in Khan Younis in early March confesses to what he did. I couldn't find a working link to the video, which is chilling: According to the monster on the screen, "the devil possessed him" when he decided to "sleep" with the kibbutz girl in her own house.

"Sleeping means falling asleep," the investigator said, in his muffled voice. "What did you actually do?"

"I raped her."

The devil may have possessed the 28-year-old "militant," who was "invited by a friend" to participate in the attack — as if it were a mere Saturday party — and received a revolver and two grenades to do it. But it wasn't immediately before he raped the girl, but rather long before that. The creature who entered the house in the kibbutz and "did what he did" (in the criminal's own words) was not "possessed by the devil": he was the devil himself, a demonic entity magically distributed among the hundreds of terrorists who participated in the attack, like a swarm of locusts.

This week, while a luxury fundraising event was taking place at Radio City Music Hall, the vigilante horde was still shouting in the streets, calling Joe Biden "Genocide Joe" — due to his now precarious support of Israel.

But it's spring in the northern hemisphere, the flowers are back on this beautiful morning, and I couldn't let you go before mentioning my creeping phlox, which is extraordinarily intense this year after seven years of hard work and care.

Happy Easter!

Six Months of Suffering

Day 184
April 7

When I despair, I remember that all through history the way of truth and love have always won. There have been tyrants and murderers, and for a time, they can seem invincible, but in the end, they always fall. Think of it — always. — Mahatma Gandhi

It's human nature: unfortunately or not, after a certain period of intense focus, all the world's situations, good or bad, lose their primacy in our thoughts.

That's what happened with this (otherwise) daily report in the last few weeks. I don't know if it was because I reached my limit, or because I finally understood that what I write or don't write has no power to change anything... Therefore, the pace of the writing has slowed down.

In this scenario, the motivation for writing ended up being reduced to "classic" milestones, like 150 days, 180 days, the death of someone, or the recovery of yet another corpse — as happened yesterday, when the IDF recovered the body of Elad Katzir, 47 — murdered in captivity before he could be released, not by the terrorists who kidnapped him, obviously, but due to some action by the Israeli government, because that's what we see happening day after day: Everything good and bad (especially bad) depends exclusively on the actions of Israel, while the responsibility of Hamas and the Palestinians is never mentioned.

Today, in theory, the motivation to write would be a milestone of this kind: dates that nobody wants to hear about, like six months having elapsed since the October 7 attacks without anything being resolved.

But when, right after waking up, I reached for my cell phone to check the news, I came across this unexpected headline in the *New York Post*: "Israeli military withdraws nearly all troops from southern Gaza, spokesperson says."

I got up immediately to access the big computer screen in the office and turn on the TV, and there it was, on every page and channel, in bold letters: "IDF withdraws ground troops from south Gaza, leaving just one brigade in whole enclave."

The reasons may vary, all of them currently being discussed by the "experts": pressure from the US first and foremost; pressure from the thousands of protesters who took to the streets in Tel Aviv over the weekend; Netanyahu's weariness (including speculation about his health and eventual death); and even advanced combat theories about changes in strategy due to the imminent intensification of the fighting on the northern border, not to mention threats of retaliation from Iran after the assassination of one of its generals in Damascus, Syria, on April 1 — the general was responsible for the distribution of funds to various terrorist groups.

I'm not in the habit of speculation, so I'll prefer to wait and see. But I honestly don't see how one can fail to celebrate this withdrawal of troops, albeit very discreetly. Even more so, it's worth celebrating the fact that, according to the IDF, 70% of displaced Palestinians are back in their homes — although I don't quite understand what homes those could be, if we believe that Israel left no stone unturned in the Gaza Strip during its incursions.

This is the crux of the matter: Much of what we know, or we think we know, differs radically from real local events, influenced by the multiple interests that guide the media, politics, and the economy. In our over-publicized era, the first victim of information overload is the truth itself, but let's leave that aside for the moment.

Have a good Sunday!

A News Story That Nobody Wants to Read

Day 188
April 11

The photo below, it seems, is a useless manifesto, a depressing waste of time and emotion based on a false hope that some hostages might still be alive in Gaza.

No one is willing to admit it publicly, but as negotiations drag on, it's becoming increasingly clear that there's no "bargaining material" available.

The latest news indicates that Hamas is unable to "provide" 40 hostages for the talks to proceed, and in recent hours, US and Israeli sources have begun to state that "some hostages were likely killed by Israeli airstrikes in Gaza, while others died due to health problems, including as a result of injuries sustained during their kidnapping on October 7."

Which immediately brings to mind the story of Hersh Goldberg-Polin, who was seen on October 7 being dragged by terrorists after his right arm had been blown off, and whose tireless mother, Rachel, traveled the world seeking support for the return of her wounded son and other hostages.

I sincerely don't know what's worse: accepting that your loved ones are no longer alive or clinging to a last shred of hope that is proving to be increasingly tenuous.

In the name of the pain these families are experiencing, I ask you, please, to find a way of bringing an end to this situation once and for all.

Hamas, however, is obviously not interested in losing this gravy train — because, from their point of view, as long as there is hope of life for these unfortunate victims, they remain in control of the situation.

Hate is a terrible feeling, but, forgive me if you can, for I hate these people with all my might. And I hope that, on their path to paradise — followed recently by the leader of Hamas Ismail Haniyeh's e three sons and four grandsons — they end up taking the wrong way and burning forever in the eternal fires of hell.

The Less We Talk, the Better

Day 190
April 13

Here at home, we've been at war with Iran for almost 20 years.

I'll explain.

Early in our marriage, after our brief, but intense encounter online, Alan revealed that he expected a war with Iran to break out soon. Very soon.

As a result, for me this story of an "imminent attack" by Iran (on Israel, not the US) started a few days ago, but for Alan it is the culmination of a long, and thankfully, fruitless wait.

Call me delusional if you want, but I still don't believe Iran will attack Israel directly. Iran is far more vile and subtle than that, and for the past 190 days it has been attacking Israel, by proxy, through its noble protégées: Hamas, Hezbollah, Houthis, the list is long and trying to enumerate them is agonizing.

If Iran wanted to attack Israel directly, it would have done so a long time ago. Those ayatollahs from hell are anything but stupid, and they are fully aware of what would happen to them if they decided to do so.

Let's be honest: We (not Israel, but the US) are the fools here for allowing this senile creature (I mean Biden) to ascend to the podium and issue a "powerful" threat to Iran consisting of a single, pathetic word: "Don't."

Does anyone really believe that this would be enough to stop an army of fanatics with near-nuclear capabilities?

The truth is that, as long as this administration is in the White House, we're all facing serious risks. There is nothing they do that doesn't go wrong, and it's been that way since Joe Biden took office — in January 2021.

Amid the growing political conflict in Israel, mainly due to the still undefined situation of the hostages — despite the equally growing rumors that they are all already dead — I watched an interview this morning with the former prime minister and current Israeli parliamentarian Ehud Olmert and, although I disagree with much of what he said, I fully endorse the advice he gave: "The less we say, the better."

What's that biblical saying again, "Silence is golden"? Especially when it comes to military strategy — a subject in which I am absolutely not an expert and, in fact, detest, but a necessary evil as you can see.

In my humble opinion, this is what's happening: Biden and his cronies are like a ship without a rudder. They don't know whether to support Israel — because the country is one of our most traditional allies and this is the right thing to do — or to attack Israel and win some votes from the boisterous, pro-terrorist mob that is becoming bolder by the day, to the point that this week, in a rally in Dearborn, Michigan, they chanted "Death to America."

Yes, you heard me. They want the death of the welcoming and wonderful country that guarantees them a free and decent existence, unlike what they would have if they decided to "follow their allegiance" to Islamic extremism while living in a country governed by it.

So, Biden decided (supposing he decides anything at all) to stir the situation a bit in order to come across as a hero, no matter what happens: If Iran attacks us, the US will save us (us, Israel); in the meantime, everyone is paralyzed, unable to assess the situation, on high alert, awaiting the announced attack "within 48 hours" that should have happened 48 hours ago.

Happy Sunday!

***

I finished writing this note precisely at 1:18 p.m. on Saturday, April 13. I hope that when it reaches the readers at 8 a.m. on Sunday, Iran has not yet attacked Israel. Because if that really happens, we will no longer have "a world as we know it today," knock on wood.

Iran, the Great Unifier

Day 191
April 14

As you might expect, the predictions I made yesterday were wrong; after all, these are opinion notes, not information notes.

Just kidding. You can trust that I do as much research as I can before writing anything, but it is true that yesterday I let my emotions get the better of me.

I also ignored that Iran, feeling an obligation to retaliate against Israel's attack on Damascus last week, had planned and published its attack plans in "every newspaper it could get its hands on" and, after the resounding failure of its mission as we shall see, hastily declared that the mission was "accomplished." Meaning, I wasn't entirely wrong.

More than 300 drones and cruise missiles traveled from Iran to Israel for over five hours, but few reached their destination. According to the IDF, 99% were knocked down without causing any damage — with the help of the US, UK, France and even Jordan, according to *The Times of Israel*.

The only victim was a 7-year-old Muslim girl, who is in the hospital in serious condition.

I know, you must be surprised that even Jordan helped defeat Iran, and that wasn't all. Saudi Arabia, Qatar, the European Union, and even China, united, decided to criticize it, not to mention that the notoriously anti-Israel UN Secretary-General, António Guterres, "strongly condemned" the attack.

Currently, the Israeli government is in a meeting to deliberate on the next steps. Biden, after a brief declaration of his "ironclad" support to the country — undoubtedly corroborated by the massive US presence in the defense of Israeli airspace — has returned to his customary position on the fence.

Of course, I'm not going to risk another prediction less than 24 hours after the failure of the previous one, but I think the world's position has become quite clear: Nobody (except for the usual fanatics and terrorists) wants to see a war between Iran and Israel that could easily result in World War III.

Let's pray.

Happy Sunday (now more likely).

Why Don't They Just Leave?

Day 192

April 15

Since I couldn't find almost nothing about it on Google, I decided to show the rest of the world what's happening here in the

US right now: Thousands of pro-Palestinian protesters in favor of the destruction of Israel and the US are blocking traffic on streets and bridges in major cities across the country, including New York, Chicago, Miami, Philadelphia, and San Francisco.

This follows the shocking public "Arabic lessons" in Chicago and elsewhere this weekend, teaching the ignorant masses to say "Death to Israel" and "Death to America" in that sacred language. Needless to say, during these lessons, they celebrated in unison, live on air, Iran's attack on Israel.

I don't know if it is mass hysteria or a collective death drive that has taken over the country, and I hope they all end up in jail, because this type of protest — blocking bridges, airports, and traffic in general — is against the law.

To these dedicated apprentices of the devil, I have a single question: Why don't y'all move to Iran or Gaza, where you will surely be loved and celebrated with your colorful hair and hundreds of gender identities? Surely in this way you would achieve your goal of self-destruction more quickly by being thrown from the tops of buildings. (For those who still don't know it, a routine way of executing homosexuals in countries devoted to radical Islam).

I hate these people.

Let My People Go

Day 198
April 21

For about two months, ever since I saw a sign that read "Dayenu" at a demonstration in Tel Aviv, I've been resisting the temptation to write an article mentioning the liberation of the Jews from slavery in Egypt, allegedly almost 6,000 years ago —

an epic event celebrated by the Jewish holiday of Passover. But now there's no escaping it: The Passover seder, the festive meal that begins the seven-day celebration of freedom, will take place tomorrow, and we still haven't seen any change in the hostage situation.

The Passover Seder has always been one of my favorite Jewish celebrations, a little less so after my grandfather's death in 1975, if I'm not mistaken. I enjoy the food, the stories told at the table, the ritual, and, above all, the singing. If you'd like to witness one of those embarrassing moments that every person familiar with modern technology has to share, you can check online my performance at a Passover seder in our house in the Atlantic Forest, Brazil, some 11 years ago (I'm now about 15 pounds lighter and my hair is about 100 times whiter).

The song I sing in the video, "Echad Mi Yodea," celebrates foundational Jewish concepts from one to 13, but I won't dwell on that because it's not my topic today, which is still to be seen: My mind started wondering, rambling through the obvious metaphor of freedom from slavery in Egypt, then on through the 10 plagues of Egypt sent by God to force the Pharaoh to free the Israelites — including the plague of locusts, easily associated with IDF's actions in Gaza over the last six months. Finally, I reached the death of the firstborns, represented by the highly targeted attacks that first took place in early April, when they killed the Iranian general responsible for allocating resources to the terrorists, while also evading the radar defenses of an Iranian nuclear facility in Isfahan last Friday.

I'll take a moment to discuss Friday's attack, which gave rise to one of the most ridiculous war propaganda events I've ever seen. As everyone knows, Iran directly attacked Israel for the first time in history on April 13, with over 300 drones, missiles, and rockets, 99% of which were shot down, an extremely embarrassing episode... for Iran. But the humiliation of the Muslim giant was only just beginning. On Friday, Israel retaliated with a strategy designed not to destroy, but to warn them: "Don't mess with us."

The rocket used as a "messenger," an icon of Israeli technology, was undetectable by radar, so it managed to reach its target intact — in stark contrast to Iran's embarrassment the previous week. This was so humiliating that, at first, Iran declared that it had been attacked and that "the response would be cataclysmic," but later decided to deny everything and claim, in a progressively shrinking sequence, that it had been just an accident, a small bomb fired internally, a bird, it had never happened.

The problem, obviously, is that there was evidence, a wreckage, photographs. The good part is that, for the moment, Iran has decided to fold its tent; let's hope they also stop showering our terrorist enemies with money and put an end to this torment.

Back to "Dayenu": One of the most exciting stories recounted through singing along the Passover seder is a list of things God has done to protect the Jewish people throughout history, each capped off by the word "Dayenu," which literally means "Enough," and I have a funny family story to tell you about this. At one of those Passover seders after my grandfather's death, my aunt was explaining the word Dayenu to her granddaughters at the Seder table and told them the meaning was "enough is enough, no more of this."

The problem is that the meaning in the song is exactly the opposite! The "Dayenu" in the chorus actually means that, even if God had only done one of those deeds — described in every verse of the song, such as, for example, "If He had given us the

Torah, and had not brought us into the land of Israel... Dayenu" — "it would have been sufficient."

Understand?

Obviously, as a tireless defender of facts, I wouldn't let that pass, so I rushed to clarify the misunderstanding immediately. My dear aunt has since passed away, years have gone by, and on that fateful day in Tel Aviv, the meaning explained by my aunt finally stuck like a tick to the word Dayenu: "Enough!"

So, this Passover, as already occurred during the holidays of Simchat Torah (there is no God) and Hanukkah (there are no miracles) following October 7, we are putting an end to the celebration of divine actions and taking justice into our own hands... But let's, nevertheless, give God one last chance to prove His existence by reinforcing the biblical warning He gave to the Pharaoh, hoping it's effective this time around: Let my people go.

Chag Sameach.

Without an Arm, but Still Alive.

Day 201
April 24

A few days ago, I published a terrible note regarding the question of whether Hamas still had [live] hostages to return.

In the text, I explicitly mentioned the story of Hersh Polin, who was last seen being dragged by terrorists with his left arm (in the note I said it was his right, for which I apologize) blown off by a grenade. Also in the text, I recalled the saga of Hersh's mother, Rachel, fighting around the world for her son's release.

Deep down, my fear was that Hersh had been dead for a long time. After all, who can withstand the explosion of an arm and other serious injuries without receiving any treatment in a decent hospital, given by a real doctor?

Hersh Polin before...

...Hersh Polin after the "extreme makeover" applied by Hamas.

So, it turns out that, in its endless quest for the most efficient and enduring torture methods in human history, Hamas published a few minutes ago a "promotional video" featuring Hersh as the protagonist: without his arm, but still alive.

The message is competing for media attention with the horrific allegation that Israel had buried hundreds of civilian victims in mass graves in Gaza — the antisemitic headline of the day in *The Times* of London, forgive me if I call *The Times* of London antisemitic, but the truth is that the newspaper has been walking a loyalty tightrope since October 7, mostly leaning toward condemning Israel based on reports that are very, very unreliable indeed.

Needless to say, *The Times of Israel* denies this news while affirming, believe it or not, that the Palestinians themselves buried the bodies and the IDF exhumed some of them "in a controlled and respectful manner" to see if they could find any hostages among them.

In a normal world, this claim would be simply unbelievable, I know. But during this war we have seen Hamas repeatedly do similar things, and much worse.

These are the people (can you call them people?) that students at major American universities are defending. Among the most recent actions, we have protest camps at Yale and Columbia... the latter, unable to resolve the situation (because they don't want to), decided to send all students home and move classes online until the end of this semester, in the beginning of May.

It goes without saying that the protesters who camped out remain right there. Several Jewish students have been prevented from entering their campus, for which they pay — imagine that —$90,000 a year.

What a world. What a life.

The Culture of Brutality

Day 203
April 26

In my note on February 14, day 131 of the Israel-Hamas conflict, I attempted to share with you an interview by Douglas Murray with Hassan Yousef, the dissident son of Hamas co-founder, Sheikh Hassan Yousef. It didn't work out well because the video was private and I don't know how many of you managed to watch it.

But today, Hassan Yousef has reached, let's say, the "mainstream," being interviewed by Jordan Peterson on an open YouTube channel that everyone can watch.

I continue to recommend that you listen to his voice, especially because of the lucidity and the clear, transparent historical context that Yousef is interested in conveying. According to his own words: "Only the truth can prevail, no matter the cost, no matter how long it takes."

And, as the writer Helen Joyce affirmed — in the aftermath of the Cass Report regarding transgender issues — we have, in a way, entered the realm of anger and revolt against the current state of affairs in the world, and today's edition with Hassan Yousef is the perfect sequence: The level of anger expressed by the peace activist has risen many degrees since his previous interview with Douglas Murray and it's about to explode.

He says so himself, self-described in the Peterson interview as a volcano about to erupt.

Don't miss it. It's a balm for the soul.

Shabbat Shalom.

Screams Before Silence

Day 205
April 28

Sheryl Sandberg is best known as the (former) powerful Facebook executive and a guru of female empowerment with her book *Lean In* (Knopf, 2013).

However, as had happened with (not) many women, Sandberg saw her focus radically change after October 7, more specifically as a result of the indifference regarding sexual abuses suffered by the victims of October 7 — shown, initially, by the lack of any expression of outrage on the part of the so-called "feminist" organizations (which, incidentally, constantly fail us women with all kinds of causes) and, subsequently, by how late these demonstrations were.

Sandberg was responsible for what was surely the most emotional of the few speeches delivered at the UN regarding this issue.

I don't like Facebook and I've never been a big fan of Sandberg's arguments in her book. Those who know me also know that being a woman has never limited me in any shape or form, and I don't need any "guide" to produce something of value in this life, but, as happened to her, I also changed my focus radically after October 7, as can be seen in the articles on my Substack, *The Middle Way*.

Sheryl Sandberg's recently released film, *Screams Before Silence*, which I haven't had the opportunity to watch (it's scheduled for tomorrow night), emerges as a mandatory document of the real events of October 7 and their repercussions.

Sandberg interviewed victims, survivors, and first responders, leaving no stone unturned while addressing the absurdity of the doubts about the intensity (and the intent) of the sexual violence perpetrated by Hamas terrorists — who continue to be defended, primarily by women, on campuses here and abroad.

Knowledge is the only true power.

The movie is available on X, free of charge.

Don't miss it.

Have a good Sunday.

Gaza in the US

Day 208

May 1

Last night, as you may know, the police were called after Hamilton Hall, the main building of Columbia University, was stormed and vandalized by pro-Palestinian, I mean, pro-Hamas, pro-terrorism "peaceful" protesters.

Don't ask me why the police weren't called to intervene six months ago because there's no good explanation for it. But yesterday, finally, it was determined that a limit had been reached; moreover, there were dozens of non-students and non-university members agitating the crowd.

As if nobody knew.

The first footage we saw from their action was simply pathetic, with police officers climbing the building's facade using an inflatable ramp and entering the room, one by one, through a small window, half-open, half-closed. But, after I turned off the TV, it seems they were super effective: In less than two hours everyone was out of the campus — protesters, campers, fighters — and the place was clear, after hundreds had been taken into custody in several NYPD buses.

The event spread rapidly overnight, crossing the country from coast to coast. At UCLA, we saw groups armed with sticks, stones, and pepper spray fighting over territory — at least that's what I heard this morning on CNN, which picked for their interview a pro-Palestinian who finally showed his face and accused the "Zionists" of attacking the "peaceful" pro-Palestinian demonstrators with weapons.

Okay, so you watch hours and hours and hours of live news showing thousands of protesters dressed as Arabs, shouting slogans, inciting violence — and CNN gives voice to a pro-terrorism activist trying to suggest that the "Zionists" were the aggressors, mind you, while in the background anyone could see the hordes of people with their faces covered by keffiyehs waving Palestinian flags.

Ironically, the situation here mirrors the reality on the other side of the world: a tiny country facing the murderous fury of millions of enemies after an unprecedented massacre took place within its territory, and the Israelis are the ones labeled as "aggressors," "genociders," and "oppressive colonizers."

Believe it or not, the ICC (International Criminal Court, The Hague, Netherlands) is deliberating whether to issue an arrest warrant for crimes against humanity committed by... Netanyahu.

Meanwhile, a new proposal for the release of the hostages is being evaluated — according to Antony Blinken, a very generous offer — but Hamas doesn't seem inclined to accept.

At any rate, I read somewhere recently that "good always triumphs." At some point, things reach an unacceptable limit and a reversal occurs. Even the seemingly invincible Third Reich was destroyed one day.

This too shall pass.

Dead and Alive

Day 214
May 7

Legend has it that on Halloween, the eve of All Souls' Day, the living are very close to the dead, making it the ideal day to communicate with them. But now we have a day and a place where the dead are even closer to the living: the negotiating table between Hamas and Israel.

When I read the news last night in an email from the *New York Post*, I thought it was an exaggeration — the *New York Post* is kind of a sensationalist tabloid type — but this morning there was no escaping it: The same news was published in *The New York Times*, a "powerhouse," so to speak, of serious journalism, albeit with strong leftist tendencies, which now means they're against Israel whenever possible.

The article was mentioned in *The Morning*, the NYT daily newsletter, right below other articles in the "ceasefire negotiations" section, where the top of the list was occupied by the information that Hamas had accepted an agreement that was "essentially" the same as the one that had been drafted during the meetings in Egypt and Qatar, despite the Israelis arguing that it was not what they had agreed to at all, and that the operation in Rafah was about to begin.

However, it seems that, while the editor was making his selection of articles, something changed, as the last on the list included the information that the 33 hostages that Hamas was promising to release in exchange for I don't know exactly what — because it's not really germane at the moment — included both living and dead.

Who could possibly stand this? Imagine the families of these hostages, held captive by violent terrorists for over 200 days, starving, never seeing the light of day, being mistreated in every way, the women and girls being regularly raped, and all subjected to immense psychological torture, believing that their country, Israel, has abandoned them and doesn't care about their suffering. I've never seen an analysis along these lines published in the media, but it's all too obvious when we see these hostages in the propaganda videos distributed by Hamas, filled with hatred for their own country and for Netanyahu.

These poor victims obviously don't have access to the facts: There's no free internet access in the Hamas tunnels, at least not for the prisoners, so they are forced to believe what they hear, while the rest of the world cheerfully adopts the stance that, if the victims of October 7 themselves are attacking Netanyahu, it's because they must be right and that's exactly what we should do — thereby corroborating the cruel lie being broadcast in the sense that Israel is a genocidal colonialist force, a popular idea these days among the "university" protesters. (I used quotation marks here because, after they were finally detained, it was discovered that more than 50% of the participants in these protests are not associated with the universities.)

It's all a lie. And these lies make the poor hostages suffer twice, as few things in this life are more painful than feeling abandoned by your own country and by everyone you love when you're in a situation of extreme need. Psychological torture, I should say.

All this considered, I'm piecing things together and coming to the conclusion that my tragic theory was correct after all: Hamas's reluctance to accept a deal is based on the fact that there aren't enough hostages to exchange, and I mean live hostages, obviously, because despite all the respect, the love, and the longing we owe to our dead, nobody will be willing to pay a very high price — in this case, the very security of Israel and its citizens — in exchange for, excuse me if you will, a bunch of corpses that have been dead for more than six months.

Again, the fate of these beloved dead is tragic, but unfortunately there is nothing we can do for them. Their duty should be to wait until this terrible war is over for the IDF to excavate the mass graves and recover them, finally giving them the dignified burial they deserve.

My God. Just writing these lines is making me nauseous, and please excuse me, but I need to throw up.

At some point I'll be back. Maybe after Israel's long-awaited offensive in Rafah is complete, not a stone left standing in those damned tunnels, and their cruel perpetrators all dead on the site, which is what they deserve: buried in mass graves, without any monument to celebrate their "heroism," forced to fend for themselves along their sweet virgins in paradise.

Is Hamas Winning the War?

Day 216
May 9

Our unusual choice of illustration for today's note is the cover story of *The Free Press* for May 9, three days before Mother's Day.

My mom must be turning in her grave.

In the image — referring to Tinder, the leading dating app in the US — the cell phone screen shows the profile of a potential "love" candidate and their "most irrational fear," "Matching with a Zionist," surrounded by kisses for terrorists and blocks for Zionists.

It's a sad (or should I say absurd) state of affairs.

As everyone knows, in war there are no winners or losers, only victims.

In the Middle East, it's difficult to know who the greatest victims are: the Palestinian children, women, and youth, displaced, without food, and in constant fear of death; or the Israeli children, women, and youth, invaded, raped, tortured, and slaughtered, not to mention those held prisoner in dark tunnels for more than six months.

But the situation is even more complicated than that. On one side, we also have the families of the hostages living between hope and uncertainty; on the other, families are being victimized — not by the manifest enemy they are fighting against, but by their own leaders, who do everything to facilitate their apparent "genocide" and, in doing so, score some extra points in the war of public opinion.

So, this is the war that the Palestinians — more explicitly, the Hamas terrorists — seem to be winning. It's a war whose greatest weapon is eliminating all nuances, variables, and complexities, reducing a thousand-year-old conflict to a black-and-white scenario: love for Palestinians and hatred for Jews, "no things considered."

This is a war in which the best weapon is not intelligence, but obtuseness.

It's not a country, Israel, that's being attacked globally, but an entire ethnic group. As you can see, Jews are being persecuted in every possible scenario, even on dating apps, as seen in *The Free Press* article "The Tinder Inquisition."

The best defense for the Jews is their own tradition, their own integrity, their refusal to surrender to age-old clichés: The oldest hatred in the world is the unconditional hatred of Jews, and, between you and me, none of these arguments are even remotely justifiable, nor will I waste my time explaining this for the thousandth time.

For those young Jewish people in search of love — who, as it turns out, are intelligent enough not to need my advice — the solution, at least for now, is to follow the prevailing playbook from my adolescence, when my mother, against my will and my immeasurable "wisdom" at the time, insisted that I should marry a Jew.

Apparently, she knew what she was talking about, and fate worked in her favor. I'm already on my third marriage to a Jew, and, as y'all know, the third time's the charm.

It's been worth every minute of the last 20 years. I just never imagined that, in a world that prioritizes diversity and acceptance of everyone above all else without question, Jews would need to close themselves off within their own community to avoid being attacked even where it matters most: the pursuit of love.

A Picture Is (Still) Worth a Thousand Words

Day 221

May 14

Many people today seem confused about which side of an issue is good and which side is evil, but the father of Shani Louk, one of the victims of the October 7 attack at the Nova music festival, has just settled the matter by attending a pro-Israel rally in Times Square.

The photo published in the *New York Post*, according to the grieving father, makes all the difference.

"And whenever you don't know who you are, you don't know: 'Am I the bad guy? Am I the good guy?' You don't know.

Look at these pictures — and it immediately straightens every-thing out."

For those who are incapable of understanding (I myself had a hard time seeing the girl's body), Shani is half-naked, face down, thrown onto the edge of the pickup truck bed like a pile of trash, her bare leg with her high-top boot hanging down with her foot sticking out.

"She died that day," the father added, making the situation even clearer to everyone.

Please check at the beginning at this entry how he would like his daughter to be remembered (photo taken minutes before the massacre, at the Nova festival).

Bodies

Day 224
May 17

Remember Shani Louk, whose lifeless body was displayed in a "parade" by the terrorists in the back of a pickup truck?

I just wrote about her three days ago. Today, 224 days after the massacre of October 7, her body, and the bodies of two other people, were recovered by the IDF in Gaza.

I'm sorry, but I had to stop everything I was doing and come here to share the news.

How else should we handle this? Now imagine the girl's fa-ther receiving her remains more than six months after she was murdered...

A question I can't control keeps running through my mind: How did these dogs from hell (sorry, dogs) keep those bodies for so long without them decomposing to a point that would hinder their identification? Do they possess some ancient Egyptian technique to preserve them so they could be "traded"? Or is it all just a huge refrigerator? A freezer, to be more precise?

The type of people we are dealing with, whom so many "good" people have been investing so much energy in defending — we already know who they are: people who rape, torture, and kill, and then keep the corpses for the "enemy" army to come and retrieve them at enormous risk, because, mind you, the IDF had to enter Gaza to recover these bodies, which were by no means "given up" voluntarily, but needed instead to be rescued as a kind of war trophy.

And this wasn't the first time.

This all happened because the infamous "genocidal" Israeli forces, yes, my friends, are capable of risking the lives of their soldiers to recover the inert and perhaps already decomposed corpse of a fellow citizen.

I apologize again for addressing and writing about these horrible things. I never thought my wit as a chronicler of everyday life would ever serve such a purpose, and the least I can do is count on your friendship and support, my dear readers, as a form of consolation.

Shabbat Shalom.

* * *

An article in *The Times of Israel*, published hours after this note, describes the encounter between Shani's parents and their daughter's body — which they say was extraordinarily well preserved. Those who wish to read the details can access it online.

The Butcher of Tehran

Day 227
May 20

I am aware that in our hyper-conscious society, where the sensitivities of each and every group, however small, must be respected to the utmost degree and valued above all else, giving malicious nicknames to a person who has just died is absolutely unacceptable and considered a serious crime. (Yesterday, for example, while working on a translation, I came across a particularly protected "gender identity" that only exists in Indonesia, "waria," which is described as follows: men who are physically men but "express their gender identity" as women.)

However, mind you, it wasn't me who nicknamed Ebrahim Raisi — the Iranian president who died in a helicopter crash yesterday morning near Azerbaijan — the "Butcher of Tehran." The nickname was given to him, according to Euronews, in the 1980s, as the holy man who "helped oversee the mass execution of thousands in the 1980s and later presided over a brutal crackdown on anti-government protests at home."

It was probably this brilliant résumé (and other unregistered details) that paved his way to the highest position in the Islamic Republic of Iran, and even more so, to the position of the likely successor to Ayatollah Khamenei, the country's current "supreme leader."

In other words, Raisi, who was only 63 years old, was, so to speak, a "figurehead," but his position as president guaranteed him a step further in the hierarchy that made him ready to replace Khamenei — who, at 85, probably doesn't have many years left.

Along with Raisi, Iranian Foreign Minister Hossein Amirabdollahian, reputed as the "coach" of Gaza's monster Yahya Sinwar, responsible for the October 7 attacks, was also dispatched to the other world.

A word of advice: Don't worry too much about respecting the names mentioned here based on politically correct demands. These are all monsters, people who don't deserve to be described as "human."

The death of two Islamic leaders in an old and poorly equipped American helicopter might be just incompetence, but it could also be a sign that there is some justice in this world, or at least that fate sometimes takes it upon itself to correct the course of history — and I'm not going to mention the various other possibilities.

Although the news media is working hard to convince us that Raisi wasn't very important and will be easily replaced, his credentials in the hierarchy of the "Republic" indicate that a fierce power struggle will keep the true leadership busy for quite some time — a leadership that would never allow the existence in the country of excrescences (oops, forgive me) like the warias of Indonesia, in stark contrast to the enthusiasm exhibited by the "Queers for Palestine" group in their demonstrations.

According to reports on social media, some people are in the streets officially mourning the untimely loss of their president, but the majority of Iranians, discreetly but not so much, are celebrating Raisi's death and setting off fireworks.

Meanwhile, the Western world remains preoccupied with gender identities, whose number, according to my translation job this weekend, is still rapidly growing. In response to my indignation regarding a fact that should simply be considered ridiculous, the AI companion I "work" with said that I have to honor this nonsense and translate it respectfully. Asked who the "Butcher of Tehran" was, Google Gemini politely replied: "I'm still learning how to answer that question."

An Intentional Reenactment of the Holocaust

Day 228
May 21

Shoes abandoned by the Nova participants who died on site on October 7, 2023.

Yesterday, I finished watching *A life*, a moving film about the story of Nicholas Winton, a young stockbroker in the City of London, who, in 1939, saved the lives of 669 children in Prague, Czechoslovakia, by "transferring" them to London and placing them in the care of temporary families before the Nazis arrived in the country.

Literally, he just stopped minutes before. The ninth and final train carrying "Nicky's refugees" was unable to leave the station, and he lamented this until the last day of his 106 years of life.

The film seems tedious at first, but from the middle to the end it is a brilliant testament to the courage and persistence of a good human being, even in the face of constant frustration.

Lately, the number of films about Nazism and the Holocaust seems to be increasing, rather than decreasing. Seventy-nine years have passed since the end of the war, and it seems we still haven't been able to fully process the horror of what happened.

I don't know if this means that in the year 2100, 77 years after the October 7 attacks, we'll still be struggling to digest the events of 2023, and I won't be around to see it. But it's already day 228 and the reactions are barely beginning to take shape.

An important element is the people — particularly journalists and photographers— who are traveling to Israel to visit the site and see for themselves what remains of the terror. One of these testimonies evolved into an exhibition about the Nova Music Festival. Not surprisingly, several photos — like the one of the shoes above — resemble the Holocaust images we have seen hundreds of times in films, exhibitions and museums.

Another photo shows a car burned by terrorists with a highly caustic chemical with the passengers inside, still alive, in a deliberate act to emulate the Holocaust — according to Reuven Fenton's account in the *New York Post* after his visit to Israel.

I recommend reading Fenton's article, not only because of the detailed description, but also for his comparison between the young survivors in Israel and their counterparts on university campuses in the United States and other countries around the world.

The lack of awareness and the robotic quality of our youth here in the US is appalling.

I hope that, by 2100, we will have been able, as a species, to overcome this stupor that seems to be afflicting us all in this *annus horribilis* of 2024.

Just for the record, this year seems to be the culmination of a nearly five-year horrible streak that began with the Covid epidemic.

Several people are predicting that a turnaround is near. Let's hope so.

Cut From the Same Litter

Day 231
May 24

As the old saying goes, "they are cut from the same litter" — an animal metaphor that's more valid in this case than ever before, oops, sorry, animals.

Some fathers teach their sons to play ball; others, like mine, teach their children how to fix things; others still try to instill values that will help ensure a better future for their offspring. So, in the case of Jamal Hassin Ahmad Radi and his son Abdallah Radi, it was no different, and lo and behold, the two decided to spend a relaxing Saturday together in Israel, raping, torturing, and killing, and probably filming it all for posterity.

It seems incredible that, no matter how much we write about October 7, we never seem to reach rock bottom: It's a bottomless pit of horrors.

This week, in addition to the father-and-son video confessing their holiday of violence to the IDF with the straightest face you've ever seen, we also had the promotional video published by Hamas showing five kidnapped female soldiers — including the currently famous (for the saddest reasons) Naama Levy — with the noble purpose of ruining their lives eternally and definitively by describing them as "women who can get pregnant."

While we delve deeper and deeper into the endless, sordid details, always counting on the committed collaboration of their proud perpetrators themselves, we always manage to find a glimmer of hope. The latest example is the emergence of a new perspective in the "Old Continent": With the election of Geert Wilders in the Netherlands and the rise of Marine Le Pen in the French polls, victories made possible by the imposing leftists' talent for ensuring the failure of all their initiatives, some people are wondering if the pendulum in the European Parliament is about to swing in our favor.

It pays to wait and see.

Shabbat Shalom.

An Epic Rescue

Day 246
June 8

This morning, Israel allowed herself the luxury of feeling joy for a few minutes and expressing it in the streets, following the daring, risky, and successful IDF operation that rescued four hostages alive and in good health from captivity in Gaza, in two different locations: Noa Argamani, Almog Meir Jan, Andrey Kozlov, and Shlomi Ziv.

That's all people are talking about on TV this afternoon.

To the family of the commander of the operation Arnon Zamora, who tragically lost his life while saving these hostages, all the families of the ones whom he saved could offer as consolation were two simple words: "Thank you."

Zamora is survived by his wife, Michal, two children, and his parents, Reuven and Ruthi.

Noa Argamani's story garnered considerable attention some time ago when her mother, a terminal brain cancer patient, made a public appeal to be reunited with her daughter before she died. We have read and heard hundreds of stories like this over the past eight months, interspersed with daring actions like this one today — not always successful, but that would look great on film, that is, on the movie screen.

Meanwhile, the usual protesters are lamenting the Palestinian victims of the IDF's heroic rescue with their usual cries of "genocide," indifferent to the suffering of these civilians who have been mistreated, tortured, and separated from their families for more than eight months, without even seeing the light of day — as Noa revealed to *The Times of Israel*. Civilians, incidentally, whose safety is the main reason for Israel's reaction, although they are rarely mentioned by the "mainstream media" and spurious organizations such as the United Nations.

Now imagine if, by some kind of miracle, the IDF managed to free all the hostages: Hamas would suddenly be left without arguments, without any "bargaining chip" to negotiate with.

Obviously, a scenario like that is impossible. Today's operation was an outlier, the result of months of planning, meticulous training, and extensive movement of troops and equipment — something that cannot be easily replicated.

Estimates reveal that there are still more than 100 hostages being held captive in Gaza.

A Moment of Truth?

Day 249
June 11

Yesterday, late in the afternoon, the UN security council (or am I supposed to capitalize that?) approved a resolution by 14 to 0 forcing Hamas to accept the agreement proposed by Israel — and supported by the US — that is currently on the negotiating table.

I'm not aware of the exact terms, but I read that it includes a temporary ceasefire and the immediate release of all hostages in exchange for the release of Palestinians imprisoned in Israel, I don't know exactly in what proportion. The three-phase agreement would ultimately lead to a definitive ceasefire, and I'm under the impression that it would eliminate Hamas's political future in a post-war Gaza Strip.

With all these elements being so vague, why did I make the decision to dedicate an entire entry to this resolution?

Let's see. Since October 2023 (and well before that), the UN has established a reputation for consistently opposing Israel. Were it not for the repeated vetoes from the United States, we would be finished. (That's me trying to spare you that other vulgar word that starts with an "f.")

I suppose you remember how long it took for the organization to acknowledge that the women who were victims of the October 7 attacks were also victims of sexual violence, I mean, extreme sexual violence, not to mention their tacit acceptance of all distorted statistics coming from the "Hamas Ministry of Health" regarding the number of victims of the war, and the subsequent forced retraction (much later), reducing the number to less than a third of the initial figure.

Finally, I imagine that, at some point, the Security Council understood that its own reputation as a representative of justice in the world would be increasingly on the line if it didn't base its proposals on reality, and it is worth remembering that this reputation is not merely a moral one. It must also be worth a great deal of money — in terms of donations and subsidies amounting to billions of dollars.

For the moment, Hamas declared that they "accept" and "welcome" the resolution. In the coming days, we will have the opportunity to understand what this truly means.

In that regard, I just had a very curious experience while watching an interview with the historian Niall Ferguson in London. The historian has an interesting personality: he's quite explosive and not at all circumspect, as one might expect from an academic intellectual.

Asked what advice he would give to a historian about to obtain his master's degree, Ferguson, after uttering a passionate defense of his point of view regarding the existence of a Palestinian state (you can imagine how that went), replied: "Don't get carried away." He then humorously added: "Like I just got carried away right now."

But that's not the story I wanted to tell. The last person in the audience to ask a question was a young man wearing a burgundy sweater, who began by saying that he agreed with Ferguson's position on October 7, but strongly disagreed when the historian affirmed that the IDF's actions had been a success.

"What kind of success is this?" the young man exclaimed, visibly agitated, "where the ratio of civilian casualties to militants is 30 to 1?" *Ill-informed*, I told myself, and Ferguson didn't let it go. "To begin with," he said, "your statistics are completely wrong. The initial ratio was 2 to 1, but soon after it became 1 to 1." And he went on, like a typical historian who knows his facts, comparing the battles in this war to others — such as the Battle of Okinawa or the attack on Dresden — where the ratio was so high, so very high, that no one even dared to publish the numbers.

The interesting thing, toward the very end of the YouTube video, was observing the young man's reaction, shown by the camera as Ferguson answered: he appeared apoplectic, increasingly close to a nervous breakdown, his hands trembling, his eyes erratic, and gnawing on his own fingers. Now imagine all those delusional protesters who continue to shout genocidal slogans in the streets being confronted in this way!

I am still cultivating two last hopes: first, that, as happened with the UN, Hamas will understand that its position is becoming increasingly fragile and will worsen if, by some miracle, the institutions responsible for issuing official opinions begin to follow the example of the Security Council; and second, that, once this terrible war is over, people will somehow be forced to reconsider their positions previously based on falsehoods and, finally, be compelled to feel ashamed of their actions.

I must be dreaming, I know. While I waste my time daydreaming, please take the opportunity to check out Niall Ferguson's lucid contribution in London, at an event promoted by an organization called "Intelligence Squared."

Music, for a Change

Day 257
June 19

"It is as if, after October 7, every day is October 7," said Suzy Weiss, the interviewer, one of my favorite people in the "new media."

Well, not exactly. Eden Golan, the singer who represented Israel in the very corny (and we now know, also very cheesy) Eurovision in Malmö, Sweden — which included the participation of the inevitable and inevitably antisemitic Greta Thunberg in protests against Israel — transcended suffering through the power of music, even if only for a brief moment of inspiration.

The strength exhibited by the Israeli singer, while facing those who tried to overthrow her, demonstrated that yes, in some way there is life after October 7 — and life always goes on.

Eden Golan is an example of the courage, and also the artistic talent of Israeli youth, who not only deserve to survive, but also to shine.

In this sense, Eden Golan is a kind of proof that no one can truly extinguish authentic brilliance, although periods of darkness might dampen it.

Am Israel chai! Enjoy!

Countdowns

Day 258
June 20

Any normal person reading the title and subtitle of this note would surely conclude that we are counting down the days until the war in Gaza ends, and that there are "only" 258 days left until this surely happens. But in the upside-down world we now live in, the meaning is exactly the opposite.

When I began my career as a columnist in Brazil many years ago, my catchphrase — quite well known, if I may say so myself — was the following: "Could the opposite be true?"

Today, that's no longer a question. Almost everything — or I would venture to say, absolutely everything, at least in certain areas of our daily lives — is the opposite of what it seems.

You know that fantastic swimmer who swept all the trophies last year but decided to stop competing this year, one "Lia" Thomas? Well, there you have it

You know that beautiful "woman" who was recently elected Miss so-and-so? Could she be he?

In the US, we have two presidential candidates this year, both reasonably old — 78 and 81, in that exact order, if you please:

• The one you saw laughing and dancing this week on TikTok during an interview with MMA fighter Logan Paul, in which his mental acuity was evident and which has already garnered 70 million hits, is considered a hateful senile monster — a "gangster," condemned by a jury of his "peers," who will "end democracy."

• The other one, seeking re-election, is at the "peak of his ability," but needed to be gently guided back by the Italian Prime Minister Giorgia Meloni after wandering off from the group of world leaders in Europe the other day. The White House issued an official statement affirming that the video had been edited to make the main "actor" appear disoriented.

So that's how things go. We have reached such a level of absurdity that one could simply relax and start laughing about it, but, unfortunately, the moment demands sobriety: What prompted my entry today was the news, published in *The Wall Street Journal,* informing us that only 50 hostages remain alive — out of the 100 everyone expected.

And this, my friends, is the countdown I was actually referring to in the title of this note.

The deadline is rapidly approaching. Meanwhile, without any basis in evidence, Hamas leader Ismail Haniyeh began declaring victory alongside his main sponsor, the Defense Minister of Iran. On the other front, Hezbollah's leader Hassan Nasrallah, also accountable to the same chief sponsor of world terrorism, began beating his own drums of war.

The attacks are coming from all sides. Time is running out. But for what, I don't know.

At least as far as public opinion is concerned, Israel seems to be screwed. Or could the opposite be true?

A Clash Between Barbarism and Civilization
Extra Edition, Day 292

July 24

It was the ultimate triumph.

I was looking for a photo of the Democrats who boycotted Netanyahu's speech in Congress this afternoon with the intention of calling them "the wall of shame," but, in the end, their absence was utterly irrelevant in the crowded room that gave Netanyahu a standing ovation more than 30 times — including the Democratic leadership sitting in the front row.

Even Elon Musk was there, in the gallery. You could barely see the empty chairs... except, of course, for the embarrassing absence of our vice president — who, according to tradition, should have presided over the session, but preferred to give a speech at some remote "fraternity" somewhere. It's not even worth commenting on.

It was thrilling to see the entire Congress chanting in unison: USA! USA! USA!

I bitterly regretted telling a friend yesterday that it was time for Netanyahu to pass the baton, and I rushed to take it back. What other leaders in the world today could have accomplished what Bibi did in Congress today?

I'm not even going to waste my time with the nonsense I heard from protesters outside the building. And for those who want to stay updated and learn the truth about Israel, the US, and the war in Gaza, I now pass the baton to the Prime Minister of Israel, Benjamin Netanyahu.

Let him speak for himself. (In a YouTube video, of course.)

Farewell, Bibas's Nanny

Day 293
July 25

Remember baby Kfir Bibas, who (in theory) turned one year old while in Hamas captivity?

Nobody has the slightest idea what happened to Kfir, his brother, his father, and his mother, all kidnapped on October 7. But today, unfortunately, we heard the news about Maya Goren, the kindergarten teacher seen in the photo above, taken before October 7, feeding the "little redhead," as the boy became known: her body was recovered by the IDF yesterday, along with four others, in a tunnel in Khan Younis, within the zone Israel declared as "humanitarian."

Now that's how it goes: 293 days have passed and all the IDF can do regarding the hostages —not for lack of will or effort — is to periodically bring some corpses back home.

According to the account from another hostage who was recently released, Hamas attempted to force the father, Yarden Bibas, to record a video against Israel while telling him how his

wife and two children had been killed by his own country's army, a claim that was not confirmed and which the IDF classified as "psychological terrorism."

These are the evil beings who were honored with fireworks and flags yesterday afternoon in Washington DC, while Netanyahu was speaking to Congress. How far can human cruelty go?

What do I mean by "human"?

To date, the alleged bodies of the Bibas family have not been recovered. The pain continues.

Heads of Snakes

Day 299
July 31

In the Middle Ages, a war only ended when the enemy king was killed on the battlefield.

The king did not remain holed up in his headquarters. Quite the contrary, he considered it a matter of honor to lead his soldiers in the fight. Killing and dying were also a matter of honor for both sides, depending on who won and who was defeated. Only the soldiers at the bottom of the hierarchy were taken, or accepted being taken, prisoner.

Killing the enemy king was known as "cutting off the serpent's head" and was a mandatory step, without which peace and tranquility could never be restored.

It's clear we're no longer in the Middle Ages and have become a "civilized" species. Except, of course, for a few people — labeled terrorists by some and "members of the resistance" by others — who believe they still live... in the Middle Ages, and thus feel entitled to kill, rape, and dismember people in the name of their failed ideology.

For these people, since we often fail to raise them to our moral level, there are times when the only remedy is to descend to theirs. With the clear objective, of course, of restoring peace and tranquility.

It's difficult to judge. But who are we to condemn?

A substantial part of history unfolds far from the public eye, and we, ordinary people, often don't know what lies behind some radical and sometimes desperate acts.

But the Mossad knows.

And I am absolutely certain that the Mossad — the world-famous Israeli secret service — knew very well what it was talking about when, perhaps, who knows, it recommended to an unnamed and unacknowledged agent that the head of the serpent that is Hamas, its "political" leader Ismail Haniyeh, be assassinated in Tehran last night, killed by a guided missile that struck him directly inside the apartment where he was staying.

Imagine this: Less than 24 hours after Israel had admittedly assassinated Hezbollah's leader Fuad Shukr in Beirut — the one responsible for the murder of 12 innocent children in the Golan Heights last Saturday.

Fuad Shukr was a terrorist wanted by the US since 1983, when he was responsible for the bombing of an American military camp, killing 241 Marines.

Haniyeh, very significantly, was in Tehran participating in the festivities for the inauguration of Iran's new "president," considered more moderate than his predecessor, who died without a rocket being fired, in a helicopter "accident."

Haniyeh did not live in Gaza and was considered a "statesman," not a terrorist. He lived in Qatar, the Hamas ally that, paradoxically, is considered the main negotiator for the hostages' release — a process that has dragged on for months without any result. To be more explicit: He lived in luxury, like a king, while his miserable subjects are dying in Gaza like flies, whether from hunger, disease, or as victims of the war itself, or because they were strategically positioned by their own leaders as "human shields."

My interpretation is that Haniyeh was a key figure who was contributing to the ongoing negotiations' constant failure. But how was he doing it, I don't know.

The Mossad knows.

The war is approaching a crucial milestone that no one would want to reach: tomorrow will mark 300 days of fighting.

It was a perfect opportunity to cut off the head of *this* serpent.

The problem is that Hamas, like other terrorist organizations we know and deplore, is not actually a serpent, but a jellyfish.

***

Update on August 1st: It's not my fault, but it has just been disclosed that Haniyeh wasn't killed by a missile, but by a bomb "planted" two months ago in the apartment where he was staying. In short, the dangerous criminal was killed by a phone!

The Rat Leaves the Basement

Day 306
August 7

Just when everyone had given up hope of ever seeing Yahya Sinwar emerge alive from the deep tunnels of Gaza... voilà: The Hamas "military" leader, known worldwide as the "architect" of the October 7 attacks — a huge insult to architects — has just been appointed by Hamas as its new political leader, with all the benefits and obligations of the position. Among them, I imagine, representing the "group" — more explicitly, the terrorist group — in the ongoing negotiations for the return of the hostages.

Has anyone stopped to think about how absurd what just happened is? This guy planned the massacre of over a thousand Israelis with extreme cruelty, including the kidnapping of over 200 people — among them young people, the elderly, and innocent children — and now he's in charge of "negotiating" their release?

What a senseless state of affairs! Putting the fox in charge of the henhouse!

At least one thing became very clear with this appointment: If anyone was still willing to be fooled by the notion that Hamas is a well-intentioned political organization, whose greatest ideal is simply to secure a small piece of land for its peaceful people — you heard about the piece of land, "from the river to the sea," although those do-gooders out there ignore what river and what sea this entails — the mask has just fallen. Forever.

It's a bit long, but pay close attention to what I'm saying: The new official Hamas leader, political figure and everything in between, the "military" leader who trained the terrorists and planned the October attack down to the smallest detail, and then went into hiding like the cowardly criminal that he is to avoid being assassinated by the country he attacked, and has remained hidden ever since, with his whereabouts unknown... are the same person!

Did you understand?

I keep talking to myself, wondering if the successful attack against Haniyeh last week in Tehran was just one step in a much longer and much more complex strategy, the second step of which would be, well, the appointment of Sinwar — because, let's face it, the truth is that the terrorist group, which considers itself the "representative of the Palestinian people," doesn't exactly have an abundance of brilliant statesmen to appoint.

I confess that, with my limited ability to foresee the future, I could never have imagined this outcome. Similarly, I have zero expectations that Yahya Sinwar might possess, hidden deep down in his despicable being, the necessary competence and generosity to "negotiate."

A natural diplomat he certainly is not. Perhaps, however, he could bring an important detail to the negotiating table: the locations of the remaining hostages, and maybe the exact number of those still alive, to put an end to false hopes. Assuming, of course, that any Hamas member, including Sinwar, is actually in possession of this valuable information.

I won't resort to the hypocrisy of wishing success to the new "leader" of my enemies, nor will I waste my time wondering if this will actually change anything. But I do have one hope: that once Sinwar has been forced out of the basement to assume his new position, he doesn't have a very long life ahead of him.

According to the Palestinian affairs analyst Ohad Hemo, Sinwar's appointment "formalized his status as 'the most powerful figure' inside Hamas," returning "the formal center of Hamas power to Gaza" in a "show of faith" by a terrorist organization "whose leadership is rapidly sinking."

Along with his inaugural speech — if there is one — Sinwar will receive the gift of a nice target on his back. He'll need a good pair of eyes in the back of his head for the rest of his life.

After all, he's the last surviving leader of the group, the last serpent's head ready to be severed to end our torment once and for all.

For Israel, Everyone Is a Citizen

Day 327

August 28

Look, you know I'm not one to mention a source without giving you my two cents, because, yes, I have an opinion about everything and I make a point of imposing it on people.

I'm also not an unconditional fan of the editor of *The Times of Israel*, David Horowitz, whom I do read regularly, but always with a degree of skepticism.

Horowitz is intelligent and obviously well-informed. He is also radically opposed to Netanyahu and makes no secret of it, not even when doing so would be a good strategy, at least as far as showing a united Israel to our many enemies — and the list is growing.

But today, my friends, in his Wednesday editorial, David Horowitz has outdone himself while parodying the absurdity of the moral and partisan attacks on Israel.

The subject was the rescue, yesterday, of hostage Farhan al-Qadi, a 52-year-old Druze Muslim who worked as a security guard at Kibbutz Magen, on the Gaza border.

Farhan was found during a search in the tunnels 326 days after being kidnapped, along with more than 200 other victims of October 7. His captors left him there alone when they fled from approaching Israelis, and Farhan said he "could hardly believe it" when he heard people speaking Hebrew on the other side of the door.

After the rescue, Farhan spoke with Netanyahu on the phone, in Arabic and Hebrew.

You simply cannot miss the parody published by David Horowitz in today's edition of *The Times of Israel*. It's mandatory reading.

May They Rot in Hell

Day 331
September 1

Remember Hersh Goldberg-Polin, the iconic hostage we wrote about in these entries on April 24?

His mother, Rachel Goldberg-Polin, an Israeli born in the US, has been for almost the entire year the most ardent defender, not only of her only son (she has two daughters), but of all the hostages held by Hamas.

Rachel spoke incessantly with presidents, congressmen, and even Pope Francis, seeking a way to force Hamas to release the hostages, always with a message of love and strength.

Speaking of which, this woman's strength is unbelievable. Her last contribution happened on the final night of the Democratic convention last month, along with her husband Jon. Rachel not only brought tears to the eyes of the crowd present at the stadium in Chicago — Rachel's and her husband's hometown — but she herself, in a gesture unprecedented until that moment, lost control and broke down in tears.

In her statement, Rachel urged her son to stay strong. "Survive!" she ordered.

I always believed that with the loss of his left arm to a grenade and without access to proper medical help or care, Hersh would probably already be dead, but let me be very clear: When Rachel came forward on Thursday, August 22, Hersh was still alive, defying all odds.

Not any longer. In today's early hours, we learned that his body was among the six corpses recovered by the IDF in a Gaza tunnel on Friday.

As we usually say here in the US, our prayers are with Rachel, Jon, and the rest of the family — as well as, of course, the families of the other murdered hostages — but, between you and me, what parent could possibly bear this?

According to the IDF, the six hostages were brutally executed hours, probably less than a day, before the IDF arrived to rescue them, before the cowards who held them captive fled their lair 20 meters below the surface of the earth.

The few hostages who are still alive probably fear the same fate: being executed just hours before their release.

The New York Times, disgusting as usual, wrote in its Sunday edition that "Israel blamed Hamas," with the phrase "brutally executed" in quotation marks.

Now you tell me: Whom should Israel blame, if not Hamas?

The newspaper probably wanted to imply that the blame falls on Netanyahu, whose most recent disappointment is being accused of showing little concern for the hostages and "prioritizing" keeping a passage to Gaza in Israel's hands. Whether that's true or not, I don't know, because the newspaper I usually read, *The Times of Israel*, is strongly against Netanyahu — as is a large part of the Israeli population, including my cousin Michal, who has been a refugee in her own country for eight months now, prevented from returning to her home on a kibbutz on the border with Lebanon, which, in all likelihood, no longer exists.

At any rate, I would certainly point to other culprits: Hamas, undoubtedly; and also the American government under Joe Biden. It's worth remembering that Hersh Goldberg-Polin had dual citizenship, so, in practical terms, an American citizen has just been executed by Hamas, and if I remember correctly, he wasn't the first. Biden is good at growling threats, "Hamas will pay dearly for this," but the truth is he's just a barking dog that doesn't bite.

If the current American government were competent and effective, this war in Gaza would have ended practically before it began, and Hamas, one way or another, would have already been eliminated. After all, if you still remember, that's what happened to ISIS during the Trump administration, although I want to make it very clear that Obama, despite his numerous flaws, didn't go easy on them either, having historically assassinated Bin Laden in an incredible operation executed by US Navy SEALs.

The Biden administration, on the other hand, only has the disastrous withdrawal from Afghanistan three years ago to be proud of. The hallmark of this administration is extreme incompetence, and if KH is elected — knock on wood — that will be the legacy we'll need to overcome.

Speaking of Afghanistan, it's worth checking out an article in *The Sunday Times* this Sunday with the daring first-person account of a woman from Kabul under the yoke of the Taliban: Currently, women are not only forced to wear black burkas and black masks whenever they leave the house, but they are also *prevented from speaking and singing even within their own homes.*

If one of these days, while walking down the street, I were to find Aladdin's magic lamp, these would be my three wishes:

• The first priority, obviously, would be the health and longevity of my husband and the safety of my son, who is currently serving in Africa.

• The second wish, if you can excuse me, would be that Trump wins the next election.

• And the third and final one, undoubtedly, would be for these Hamas terrorists, from the leadership to the rank and file, to all rot eternally in hell, which is where they belong.

What Is an Agreement?

Day 333
September 3

Yesterday, in Jerusalem, Hersh Goldberg-Polin was buried at a funeral attended by thousands of people. The day was also marked by demonstrations in Tel Aviv that involved hundreds of thousands of people.

Several protesters were interviewed by the media, and all of them, without exception, blamed the Israeli government for being unable to reach an agreement with Hamas up to this point.

Tensions are rising daily, and understandably so. Relatives of hostages still held by Hamas are expressing a perfectly justified sense of urgency, such as the brother of another iconic hostage, Naama Levy, who told the reporter that with each passing day, the possibility increases that his sister will end up being executed, as happened to the six victims over the weekend.

It is true. News to that effect is already out there. But what left me angry and heartbroken is that no one, not a single person being interviewed, took into account that an agreement, whatever it may be, is not under the total control of Israel or of the increasingly hated Benjamin Netanyahu.

No one has even suggested that Hamas — Hamas, I repeat — has absolutely no interest in reaching an agreement... and that is why the agreement is not happening, not because of Netanyahu.

Biden has already raged at will, trying to "force" Hamas to sign something, but we already know how his decisions are usually "respected": Nobody cares what Biden and his cabinet members say or don't say.

The situation is very serious.

Try to put yourselves in Hamas's position: The terrorists hold all the cards! The more they try to delay the return of the hostages — considering that, as we've already speculated, they may not even know where all these "hostages" have been for so many months — the greater the likelihood that they will win this war.

But don't ask me, because I don't know. Moreover, I'm afraid to know what a "Hamas victory" would mean.

Consider this week, for example, the astounding effect of the summary execution of six hostages with a shot (or multiple shots) in the back: Thousands of demonstrators continue, amazingly, to demonstrate in favor of the terrorists in the major capitals; the summer break ended yesterday, and on the campuses of the largest universities, once again teeming with radical students, it seems time has stood still.

Plus ça change, plus c'est la même chose.

In Israel, on the other hand, the population is getting, understandably, increasingly desperate. But against Hamas? No. Against their own government, and their own country.

The more time passes and nothing is resolved, the more divided the country becomes, and the more the capacity for thoughtful actions is radically reduced, supplanted by the constant pain of a stab in the heart repeated countless times.

Now imagine the opposite situation: Let's say that next week an agreement is reached, the hostages who are still alive and the bodies of those who did not survive are returned, and a ceasefire is implemented.

What will be left for Hamas?

A wasteland and its swift oblivion by public opinion, which will have nothing left to shout about.

The much-lauded "two-state solution" will also enter a state of suspended animation, because everyone involved is aware that, at the moment, no talks are feasible.

Several years will pass. I see no signs that Hamas will be eliminated by other means as part of a broader agreement, and the "leaders" of the "movement," whose bank accounts are replenished daily by donations and incentives from institutions around the world, will see their resources dwindle.

Israelis, on the other hand, will reinforce their security, bury their dead, and, because there is no other humanly possible solution, will move on with their lives, gradually recovering their talents and capabilities that, before the war, positioned the country among the most important in the world, despite being so small.

It's not hard to understand why Hamas has absolutely no interest in any of this; any eventual agreement would be the final blow to its murderous ambitions.

Now, all of this, obviously, is just an exercise in speculation. If I really knew what to do and what the solution would be to end this terrible war, whose first anniversary is only 23 days away, I probably wouldn't be here writing these notes for you, but what if... um... the whole world stopped giving all sorts of incentives for Hamas to maintain this situation, then maybe... right?

And then I woke up.

The Explosion of Pagers
Extra Edition, Day 347

September 17

For several hours the world has been talking about nothing else, and obviously this is not about the second assassination attempt against Donald Trump.

It is, in fact, about the most daring counter-terrorism operation the world has ever seen: the simultaneous explosion of pagers belonging to Hezbollah terrorists, resulting in several fatalities and thousands of injuries across Lebanon.

Hezbollah blamed Israel and swore revenge.

I accept the blame. Who else, after all, would have the creativity and the technological skills to execute such an action? With such precision?

Until this morning, this could only happen in a movie, as, incidentally, in the incredible *Kingsman: The Secret Service* — which, coincidentally, I watched last week.

Let's face it: With all the technological advancements and increasingly terrifying weapons, life is increasingly imitating fiction.

This week, I'm suffering "in installments" through the terrifying information provided by Annie Jacobsen, the expert on weapons of mass destruction who has just released a book including interviews with several highly confidential sources of information, which should never be shared with the public.

Yes, my friends, the world is getting deeper and deeper into the Twilight Zone.

Now, whether all this will ultimately take us to the end of the war or the end of the world, I don't know.

Weight Without Measure

Day 352
September 22

In yesterday's edition of *The New York Times* newsletter, celebrating the arrival of autumn, a brief note in the "Other Stories" section reports the following:

"An Israeli airstrike on Lebanon killed a top Hezbollah commander. Lebanese officials said the bombing leveled two apartment buildings and killed at least 14 people."

The note does not name the commander, Ibrahim Aqil, Hezbollah's head of operations and commander of the Radwan Division, an elite force roughly equivalent to the American Navy SEALs. Naming the culprit in this case would imply that the "victim" was a criminal wanted by the American government since 1983, when he was responsible for an attack on the American embassy in Beirut that left 63 dead, and another on a US camp that killed 241 Marines, which I have already mentioned.

The reward offered for his capture — established by the State Department in 2023, on the 40th anniversary of the attack — is

$7 million, but for *The New York Times*, what really matters are the 14 who died during Friday's attack. The newspaper, apparently, takes advantage of the proverbial short memory and ignorance of history on the part of the general public to advance its relentless agenda against Israel... and rack up a few more clicks.

The rap sheet for Ibrahim Aqil, who was around 64 years old, also includes the kidnapping of Americans and Germans and the transformation of an insignificant militia — the original Hezbollah — into a powerful political, military, and terrorist organization, not necessarily in that order. His most recent plan was to conquer Galilee — the small corner of the world in northern Israel where I was born — with an attack that already had a set date.

Along with Aqil, two other high-ranking commanders were "dispatched," together with the unfortunate 14 people who were in the building at the time of the attack — yes, 14 of them compared to 300 of ours, Americans no longer remembered by anybody — except, of course, the surviving Marines and the families of the deceased.

Fourteen, to be honest, was not that much.

According to the panel above published yesterday, only three members of Hezbollah's command line remain to be "eliminated," including the leader Hassan Nasrallah — the organization's "secretary-general" — whose death would have an immeasurable impact on the region. None of those assassinated so far were of his stature.

Now, the problem with all of this is that this offensive in the North seems to foreshadow an intensification of operations on the Lebanese border. A war against Hezbollah, according to high-level people in the intelligence community, would be at least 30 times larger than the war against Hamas, especially considering the 150,000 rockets and missiles stocked by the organization.

Who in their right mind would want to stick their hand in this hornet's nest?

Perhaps a country that has been attacked daily by these missiles for more than 11 months... not to mention the entire population of the region that has been evacuated to other locations, including my cousin whom I already mentioned and who has been out of her home for 11 months, living in a borrowed apartment, along with thousands of other "refugees in their own country."

Last week, the Israeli government declared that Hamas's military force had been completely dismantled, but the thorn of the hostages in captivity continues to prick. Our biggest ally, the United States, seems to have temporarily given up on us and has just declared that there will probably be no further attempts at an agreement while Biden is in the White House... wait a minute.

Americans might be busy and neck-deep in the presidential election campaign, but I shudder to think that we'll have to wait another 45 days until the elections and another 75 until the inauguration of the new president (I don't even want to think about the possibility of suggesting the wrong gender for the new occupant of the White House) before we can "talk" again about the release of the poor, wretched hostages who manage to survive that long.

We're between a rock and a hard place.

Have a good Sunday.

A Silent Campaign

September 24

I can't be really sure, but I could say without much hesitation that the Democrats are perfectly aware that their policies are extremely unpopular with the vast majority of Americans.

If that weren't the case, what would be the reason for the impeccable Kamala Harris (I'm being ironic, obviously) to radically change her past opinions for which she is criticized, such as her radical opposition to fracking, a technique essential to the economy of Pennsylvania, which currently sits at the top of the list as the most crucial state for victory in the Electoral College?

The list is long. With regard to each item included, KH did a complete 180 and then simply stopped talking about it.

I suspect that a reason why the candidate doesn't give interviews or participate in press conferences where she would be prevented from using a teleprompter isn't exactly her inability to answer difficult questions — we saw in the debate with Trump that she's quite capable of handling that — but rather that it's difficult to lie with the most smug face in the world and, on top of that, convince everyone that she's telling the truth.

As you may know from your own experience, this is a rare talent, albeit common among successful politicians.

Take me, for example: In a situation like that, I would inevitably let slip some inconvenient point of view without the slightest effort.

Because of this strategy, with each passing day, from now until the elections, the pressure decreases a little, as it's one less day for the candidate to face this tremendous and constant predicament that her leftist past imposes on her.

And this doesn't apply only to the head of the ticket, but also to Tim Walz, the vice-presidential candidate, who has a history of even more controversial opinions hated by the vast majority of Americans.

Their campaign is betting on the short memory, lack of curiosity, and lack of time of voters in general, and is getting a little help from the media, which methodically obscures the thorniest controversies as if they never existed.

Regarding one of those "cancelled" controversies, my memory was refreshed yesterday afternoon while watching the Fox Nation series *Transfixed*, hosted by Riley Gaines, a former athlete and victim of the progressive policies involving women's sports.

After losing some medals and trophies to a male swimmer known as "Lia Thomas" — let me repeat: a male swimmer — Riley quickly bounced back and became an activist and now a TV presenter, two roles in which the former athlete excels.

The new "darling" of the conservative media reminds us of the sheer horror implied by this "medical experimentation" to which so many young people — including minors and children — have been subjected, more intensely since the advent of Covid, with touches of cruelty that evoke the experiments of Josef Mengele, the infamous Nazi doctor.

During this electoral season, the issue has completely vanished from the media, along with all its nuances and the ridiculous attacks on everyday grammar (remember the crazy pronoun system everyone was forced to follow?), and you don't need me to explain why. Anyone with a modicum of common sense can see the serious danger these "progressive policies" represent for the future of humanity.

That alone, let's be honest, justifies all decent people voting for Donald Trump and his vice president JD Vance next November.

We Will Dance Again

Day 357
September 27

This morning, my friend and "informant" from Florida, who luckily is currently visiting Brazil far from Hurricane Helene, which is threatening her region, updated me on the "local news," and I'm not talking about the olive oil protected by a locked cabinet in a supermarket in Rio, but about the chilling statement by the "leader" of a "leftist" party called PSTU, who this week made a statement in favor of Hamas at an event of the so-called "Arab Palestinian Federation of Brazil."

Look, I'm not talking about a statement in favor of the Palestinian people. I understand that some people believe that the Palestinian people are an oppressed people — and they are, but not by Israel — which automatically makes them fit the victim-in-need-of-protection stereotype that the "left" has adopted gladly and voraciously in recent years, but still, that's not what this is about.

The so-called "leader" of the party was quite explicit when he said he was speaking on behalf of "a left-wing party that is not ashamed to say it belongs in the same trenches as those who carried out October 7." (I made a point of not adding my opinion by emphasizing the statement with quotation marks as usual; instead, I reproduced the so-called "declaration" verbatim.)

I can't help but wonder: Did he really mean that he belongs in the "same trenches" as those who raped, tortured, played soccer with severed breasts, cooked babies in ovens, kidnapped, and committed other acts that we thought no human being would be capable of, all with extreme violence, and on top of that, recorded everything on video to proudly post it on social media and keep it for posterity? Is that what's happening?

I'm sorry, but, being very naive, I can't believe that this young person, looking like a good family man with a keffiyeh around his neck, as well as several people in the audience who enthusiastically cheered his speech, would actually want to be on the same planet as these Hamas terrorists, let alone in the same "trenches."

The ignorance of these people is astounding. Hamas doesn't even have trenches; quite the opposite: it has an extensive and extremely expensive network of tunnels 30 meters below the surface of the earth, built with money that "good" people like this imbecile donated to the "Palestinian people."

Now, I'm not here to condone ignorance and stupidity. Instead of lining up with these cruel murderers, the likes of which have rarely been seen in history since Genghis Khan, these useful idiots captured by "leftism," just like their leader, who was democratically elected president of Brazil, equally ignorant and stupid, should be better informed about what they are declaring in public.

Even Muhammad himself, had he lived in the 20th century and witnessed the Holocaust, would have hesitated to share a "trench" with these disciples of Hitler who, to be fair, gloriously surpassed the wickedness of their inspiring master, but what am I saying? These terrorists probably never heard of Hitler; they are simply following the playbook of their local imam, who educated them from birth to hate Jews — I mean, "Zionists."

Osvaldo Aranha — the legendary Brazilian diplomat who presided over the UN General Assembly that gave rise to the State of Israel — must be turning in his grave.

Honestly, I never thought Brazil could go so low. What a shame, my goodness.

But let's change the subject now, because nobody can survive in this life without recovering from trauma and suffering, and the title of this note (*We Will Dance Again*) and the accompanying video of the same name are a moving account of Israelis who are doing just that: Almost a year after the event and with 30% of the hostages still in Hamas's hands with no date set for their release, they are overcoming their pain and transmitting a message of hope, despite the millions of imbecile "leftist" militants scattered around the world who would prefer they didn't exist.

Shabbat Shalom.

Sinwar, Gone.

Day 377
October 17

The news has just arrived, and the IDF is still analyzing the DNA and other signs for final confirmation, but everything indicates that we finally "caught" Yahya Sinwar, the "architect" of October 7.

Poor architects, again, mentioned in the same sentence as this monster of historic proportions.

In an excellent interview with Bari Weiss the other day, Douglas Murray explained that Jewish law dictates that "we should not delight in the death of any human being." And he quickly added, "I am not Jewish."

Well then: I am Jewish, but today, God will have to forgive me for transgressing this law.

That was wonderful, IDF!

It took a while, but you sure did it!

The victims of October 7 and all the Jewish people are indebted to you.

The Attack on Tawaki Torquay

Day 395

November 4

There's a video circulating and being widely shared on social media, and this doesn't concern me at all. Right?

Well, not really. More or less.

Since my time as a professional translator is fading rapidly and I stubbornly need to keep making money in order to survive, I've recently started to work "training" LLMs, the famous "Large Language Models" that are being used, among other things... to replace translators. And also, transcribers, and stenographers, and an undetermined multitude of other people who fundamentally work with language — you know, those highly ignored and undervalued skills that unduly claim to be responsible for the existence of civilization and the survival of humans.

Just a small, insignificant thing.

One of the most unfortunate "coincidences" of this new line of activity is that a good portion of the texts and audios I analyze are against Trump — an issue that will possibly disappear in the near future — and, worse, much worse: against Israel and against the Jews.

What can I do? I need to eat, I'm a competent professional, I'm also honest, so I hold my nose, swallow hard, and move on, translating and correcting a torrent of lies that would make any normal person throw up.

Yes, I am thus contributing to the ignorance in the world. I must confess that I still haven't been able to decide how to act and what to do about it, but yesterday I came across something that I can hardly describe... I'll describe it to you.

The task was to create an audio transcription and subsequent translation into Portuguese, both done by AI, which I was supposed to correct.

The problem is that it's all very bad and often totally incomprehensible, so what can a tiny little human being do, isolated in her little office hidden in front of her screen, to stop the march of these absurdities and still keep her job?

The text read as follows (with errors): "Children have died. The pager and Tawaki Torquay attacks. Of course they were targeted at Hispola fighters but you didn't know who's who was going to be in the room..."

The argument, of course, was that Israel is a genocidal country that is decimating millions of people without any criteria and should be... Condemned? Demoralized? Eliminated? Erased from the face of the Earth as if it had never existed?

I could have quickly become consumed by the merits of the issue and the outrage it provokes in me, but like a good little slave fighting to survive, what really happened was that, in the several minutes that followed, I was obsessed with "Tawaki Torquay." What kind of attack was that, one that no one had ever heard of? Was it a city? The name of a hospital?

I dug and dug deep, and all I could find on Google was an Instagram post with a photo, written in Arabic, no less: an interview being broadcast to millions of people, shaping the opinion of millions of people and creating this imaginary place where Israel was carrying out its genocide of the day.

Of course, the second thing I did was to ask "my" AI. When in Rome, do as the Romans do, right?

My AI told me it must be a misunderstanding, a spelling mistake, because there was no place, city, hospital, or school in Gaza, Lebanon, or, excuse me, in the middle of fucking nowhere, called "Tawaki Torquay."

To make a long story short, this short, insignificant human being, who doesn't know the meaning of the expression "give up," after wasting a lot of time on the question, finally saw the "light," helped by the word "pagers" that preceded the enigma: "Tawaki Torquay" was, in fact, "walkie-talkie."

My God! This was actually referring to the absolutely incredible Israeli action that exploded hundreds, no, thousands of pagers and walkie-talkies used by Hezbollah terrorists throughout Lebanon, on September 17.

Look, I'm only writing this note today because, if I didn't, the infamous case of the "attack on Tawaki Torquay" would disappear from sight, swallowed up in the multitude of data circulating on the internet and on my desk every single day.

But this case raised a red flag: Everyone is going all in on this artificial intelligence business, all the companies are ditching humans and replacing them with this technological wonder... which works exactly as you just saw depicted above.

Furthermore, to use a popular saying that would probably drive AI crazy, everyone is "as lost as a nun on a honeymoon."

Go figure.

My panic intensified even further when I was reminded, while reading *The Free Press* this morning and researching online, that Kamala Harris was named the United States "AI czar" last July. The woman is in control of the direction AI is taking and is probably doing the same thing she did in her previous "czar" role, controlling the border. That is: nothing, zilch, nada.

Now connect all the dots and you might understand even better why, whenever one asks AI who Kamala Harris is, AI always responds with lavish praise, while with Trump you already know how this goes.

So tomorrow, this monument to incompetence, who has already done far more damage to the world than we can imagine, might be elected president of the United States.

Perhaps, due to my high level of anxiety, I'm just creating a crazy conspiracy theory based on one or two factors from my personal experience, and everything will turn out all right in the end. Or perhaps there is a God, and he is currently planning to save us from this new and hyper unstable Tower of Babel, among so many other evils that are currently afflicting a humanity that's making Sodom and Gomorrah seem like an amusement park.

It doesn't hurt to have a glimmer of hope.

After all, something, or Someone, saved Donald Trump's life three months ago in Butler, Pennsylvania, when the president turned his head to look at a picture at the exact moment the bullet that would have killed him was fired from the rooftop across the street.

Danger Zone

November 8
73 Days

Democrats are heartbroken, and that's not all. They are also surprised — and shocked. How could their spectacular DEI candidate, a woman of color, with no other qualities, not win this election?

They didn't expect that the overwhelming majority of Americans would hate so much the radical proposals they forced us to live with for the last four years. And I mean forcing openly, of course, because covertly, in the dark backrooms of society, a form of radical Marxism had already been brewing... since when, the 1960s?

The last four years were merely a window of opportunity for them to stick out their "progressive" little heads... only to have them cut off, lol.

I believe there are still many more people in this country who detest them, who otherwise haven't been able to overcome the heavy-handed propaganda to the point of voting for the "enemy."

Once the euphoria has passed, there's so much we need to undo. We don't even know where to begin, but a good example of the current mood could be seen in Greg Gutfeld's monologue on *The Five* yesterday.

What we certainly cannot do is relax. Given the immense shadow of Trump, elected by a vast majority, preparing to govern, the radicals will surely go crazy and do everything they possibly can to breathe the last breath they have left, which puts the country and the world dangerously on the brink of a precipice for the next 73 days.

It has already begun. This morning, Israeli football fans were cowardly surrounded and attacked in the streets of Amsterdam by pro-Palestinian demonstrators, in what the Israeli government described as a "modern pogrom." Ten people were injured and hundreds of others were "besieged" in hotels.

The Netherlands — who would have thought! The homeland of Anne Frank, and a hub of modernity and freedom, no less!

Europe declared itself "deeply embarrassed" by this shameful display of antisemitism, but the truth is that, since October 7, hating Jews has become permissible again.

Netanyahu and El Al sent planes over to bring the fans back to Israel free of charge. All the victims were released and treated in hospitals.

No vigilance will be excessive during this time of transition. Next year, perhaps, we will finally be able to demonstrate that, in order to have a "free Palestine," its citizens will need to rid themselves of Hamas, not Israel.

Shabbat Shalom.

Ceasefire in Lebanon
Extra Edition, Day 417

November 26

In a televised address less than five minutes ago, Netanyahu declared that Israel will be signing a 60-day ceasefire with Hezbollah on the northern border.

The agreement being presented to the Knesset (the Israeli parliament) right now acknowledges the progress made in dismantling the terrorist organization and also aims to "isolate" Hamas.

The details are currently unknown, but also irrelevant.

Any effective move to reduce the war effort and the growing number of casualties is welcome.

Trump Lays Down the Law

49 days, 19 hours, 59 minutes and 55 seconds
December 2

I'm so shocked by the news that I had to write about it in two languages — only English wasn't enough to contain my outrage.

Being an American citizen since 2018, I recently started not only to write in English, but also to feel the "urgency" to write arise in English. Today, however, I was forced to also write in Portuguese to better understand my feelings.

This morning, a hostage who had been considered alive until today was declared killed by the IDF. His parents had been demonstrating for their son's release at every possible opportunity, including the Republican convention on July 17, and for the last time... yesterday.

The kidnapped boy — I am forced to refer to him as a "boy" because he was only 21 years old — was an idealist who had enlisted as a volunteer with the IDF and was the commander of a tank in Gaza that was the target of a bomb attack.

The video of the tank catching fire and the terrorists leading the soldiers into captivity went viral on social media. Two of them had already been declared dead beforehand, and this morning it was Omer Neutra's turn.

Did you understand? Have you reflected on this? Omer was killed on October 7, and his body was held "hostage" in Gaza for 423 days! And during all that time, his parents never lost hope...

How far can human monstrosity go?

But what am I saying? Human? These terrorists don't deserve to be called human; even "animals" is too good for them, and I repeat myself.

So, just a few minutes ago, Trump declared that he will turn the lives of these animals into a living hell if ALL the hostages are not released by January 20th, the date of our new president's inauguration.

A lot can still happen before then. For now, Biden is revealing his true intentions in homeopathic doses, for example, by pardoning his son Hunter's crimes after having spent years saying that he wouldn't.

Honestly, after dropping out of the race and choosing Kamala Harris to replace him as a candidate, it seems that Biden is on a mission to destroy the Democratic Party from within.

Now, that's their problem. As you can probably tell (and if you can't, just check the subtitle above), I'm counting down the days until I see them all gone for good.

Needless to say, they won't be missed.

Let There Be Hanukkah

Day 437
December 16

In December 2023, we read the following line on a social media post published in Israel: "On Simchat Torah, we learned that there is no God. On Hanukkah, we realized that there are no miracles."

I still cry when I read this.

You must remember that, last year, Simchat Torah — a joyful holiday that celebrates the completion of the annual reading of the Torah — fell on October 7. I still shiver and get emotional as if living it all over again. When Hanukkah, the "Festival of Lights," arrived, the war was underway and there was no hope of getting the hostages back in sight.

It was a tragic period, the year in which we lost faith — and it still is.

Since then, about 60% of the hostages have been released, others have been declared dead, and an uncertain number still remain in the hands of Hamas, which just last week refused to inform their names.

A long war has been fought since October 2023. Many people have died. Antisemitism, once considered unacceptable, became prevalent in the so-called civilized world, including in Brazil, where I grew up with nothing to fear.

However, after more than a year, we can say that some miracles have indeed been performed. Hamas is mostly dismantled. Hezbollah was practically decimated via exploding electronic devices and a handful of unbelievable assassinations. And last week, after almost 14 years of a brutal civil war, the Assad regime was defeated in Syria.

As a result of all these events, the previously all-powerful Iran, somewhat enabled by the support of Biden's administration, now appears weak and defeated, with their "proxies" mostly gone.

Still, while all of this was going on, the hostages, who were the primary motive for Israel's war, remained an unresolved issue. The constant refusal by Hamas makes us wonder if they even know where the remaining victims are. So, it was with a lot of hope in my heart that I read in *The Times of Israel* that our *de facto* president, Donald J. Trump, had a call with Bibi Netanyahu on Sunday to discuss their release.

In these last few weeks after the election, we have seen the world change fast before our very eyes as a result of Trump's victory, even before his inauguration, which, for some of us, also feels like a kind of miracle. And now we hear that, before Trump takes office, a hostage deal is near and will probably happen next week, just in time for our faith to be restored by a new Hanukkah miracle.

This year, we have a rare and beautiful coincidence happening, as the first candle of Hanukkah falls on Christmas Eve.

Let there be light. Let there be Hanukkah again.

Happy Holidays.

This Was No Luxury Resort

Day 451
December 30

I wish I could have ended the dreadful year of 2024 without writing this post, but I couldn't.

It wasn't enough that I was wrong about my hope for a total release of the hostages and a new Hanukkah miracle. Hanukkah came and went, yet no merciful God made Himself manifest in the 21st century.

And that was not all. Yesterday, we were rewarded with the news of a gruesome report being prepared by the Israeli Ministry of Health to be presented to the United Nations, containing everything you and I hoped did not happen — after seeing some of the hostages released in November last year in apparently good conditions, that is, not starved, not tortured, not sexually abused.

In other words, looking intact.

They were deliberately starved. As a mitigating factor, they were overfed to not appear too squalid upon their release to their families.

They were tortured. They were subjected to several kinds of torture, from being branded with a hot iron to undergoing surgeries and painful, unskilled medical treatments without anesthesia.

They were sexually abused. The abuse included forcing teenagers to undress and perform sexual acts on each other while the terrorists whipped their genitalia.

They were not intact. They were subjected to humiliation, kept in the dark with very little food for days, and forced to defecate on themselves.

Some will never recover. Some killed themselves a few months after being released. Others died months later as a result of their suffering and lack of medicine during captivity.

And I'm sure this is not all. There are still 105 hostages being held by Hamas, among them 34 corpses. Seven of them are Americans.

Now multiply these atrocities suffered by the hostages released a year ago by 365, and we will barely touch the surface of what might have been happening to them all this time.

Trump promised us that Hamas will have "all hell to pay" if all of those hostages are not free by inauguration day. This allows the torturers and their victims to respectively inflict and endure another 22 days of extreme pain.

As for the UN, I can't help but be curious about their reaction to this newly released document. Let's see if they can still find a way to defend Hamas as "a persecuted Palestinian people subjected to genocide by Israel."

***

It seems unlikely that I've been allowed to use ChatGPT to edit this book. Well, not anymore. In this last entry of 2024, the "system" refused to edit this entry with the following commentary: "This content may violate our usage policies." Of course, there was nobody "there" to tell me if reality and real facts "violate" their policies. Shame.

Part Three

2025

Dai!

Day 467

January 15

Breaking news reports that an agreement has been reached with Hamas to release the hostages.

"Dai!" says the sign, in Hebrew, shown by a woman in a wheelchair at the demonstration in Tel Aviv. Enough!

It's more than enough already. Simply unbearable.

The deal is not what one would expect to avoid "all hell breaking loose": Only 33 hostages are part of the first "installment;" of those, only 23 are supposed to be alive. Which of them are alive is anyone's guess, as this is another torture tactic employed by Hamas to torment us.

Each of us has our own "favorites" — among them the then-newborn baby who was taken with his mother and brother, Kfir Bibas. As you might remember, Kfir "celebrated" his 1st birthday in captivity, on the 104th day of this nightmare.

Yesterday I read in *The Times of Israel* that "Trump envoy swayed Netanyahu more in one meeting than Biden did all year."

No wonder.

Please don't buy Biden's lies throughout his "farewell speeches," the last and most official of which is supposed to take place tonight in primetime. I don't give Joe Biden an inch of the benefit of the doubt. His inaction is responsible for a great part of the pain these October 7 victims had to endure.

Are the Palestinians Refugees?

Day 478
January 26

Outrage is rising as President Trump asked Jordan and Egypt to take in Palestinians in order to allow reconstruction in a devastated territory.

"Ethnic cleansing!" yelled Al Jazeera.

"We're not going anywhere," said an enraged Gaza citizen.

But you can't have it both ways. Either you are a refugee or a citizen, and the whole Palestinian argument — not to mention the billions of dollars they receive and the UN offices located in their land — is based on the fact that they are indeed refugees.

Therefore, if they are, it is only fair to ask their countries of origin to take them back as an act of "justice."

Isn't it?

QED.

The Bibas Family Is No More

Day 483
January 31

Like many who are keeping track of the hostages, I have been worrying and praying for the return of the Bibas family.

We celebrated Kfir Bibas's 1st birthday while he was in captivity, and believe it or not, we also celebrated his 2nd birthday, still in captivity.

But this morning, when I read that the list of hostages to be freed in the next "batch" on Saturday included only men, and among them was Yarden Bibas, Shiri's husband and Kfir's and Ariel's father, it marked the end of all hope.

If we're moving on to men, it means that all women and children alive are already out.

Reading the TOL article, I realized that "Hamas has claimed that Shiri and the two boys were killed in captivity" back in 2023, allegedly by Israeli bombing.

Hamas lies. But in this case, unfortunately, all signs indicate that we have been fooling ourselves for more than a year while celebrating the lives of these unfortunate victims.

I hope I'm wrong, but probably not.

Bibas family, Z"L.

Shabbat Shalom.

An Unexpected Outcome
History Made Live

February 5, Day 488

Have you ever been to the wonderful Club Mediterranée Gaza by the deep blue waters of the Mediterranean Sea?

Neither have I. It doesn't exist.

What we have in Gaza at this moment, after almost a century of refugee camps gradually replaced by an unruled and overpopulated mass of buildings, followed by almost 500 days of war, has become scorched earth.

As President Trump reminded us of last night in the press conference with Netanyahu, there is not one building left standing and it's not a livable place.

I have been expecting Trump to come up with an unusual solution. After all, in his previous administration he transferred the American embassy to Jerusalem, declared Israeli control of the Golan Heights, and, last but not least, celebrated the creative and unexpected Abraham Accords between Israel and a few Arab countries — a feat previously deemed as impossible.

This is a man who makes a living by thinking out of the box, a quality that his many detractors profoundly resent.

What they hate more than anything is that Trump is usually right, and usually succeeds in his daring endeavors, like earlier this week (yes, it's only Wednesday morning in America), when he imposed sanctions on Canada and Mexico only to suspend them shortly after, as Trump and our neighbors quickly reached an agreement.

Wicked!

On the very same day that our president withdrew the country from the corrupt UN Security Council and UNRWA, which, let's face it, are hardly more than incubators for terrorists, there he came with the unique idea of rebuilding Gaza as the "Riviera of the Middle East."

For those with a developed sense of imagination, it was not difficult to come up with such a revolutionary project, considering that Gaza, underneath all that rubble, is nothing less than a wonderful stretch of land by the ocean.

It reminded me of a very mean joke we used to tell about Brazil: "God was chatting with a few friends from several countries, each lamenting their own national troubles, except for the Brazilian, who seemed very proud and happy. So the envious friends inquired of God why on earth He decided to create Brazil in such a beautiful location, with luxurious forests, and mountains, and white sandy beaches, and a wonderful climate all year long. God answered in a conciliatory mood, and advised them wisely: 'Wait until you see the little people that I'm going to put there!'"

Of course, this is just a joke, an outrageous joke like all good jokes. The Brazilians are in fact a very nice people, as I'm sure, given the chance, the Palestinians could be, once they are freed from those horrible, monstrous beings who have been governing them for a few years in a reign of terror and fear.

And the man to give them this freedom, mind you, seems to be Donald Trump.

The day today — and especially this press conference — was so packed with news and information that the only way you can keep up to date is by watching them unfold live.

Trump's proposal for Gaza is to temporarily take over the strip, move the residents to neighboring countries, dismantle the unexploded bombs, clean the rubble, and rebuild it as a wonderful place where people from all over the world, including Palestinians, will be able to enjoy peace, beauty, and quality of life.

A veritable dream!

Before I wake up, I will just wrap it up with a crazy idea that came to my mind out of nowhere, while listening to the president last night: Jared Kushner, Trump's son-in-law, dedicated the last four years to developing luxury resorts in unusual places, the latest of which was approved in Albania just two weeks ago.

Now, all you need to do is connect the dots, *et voilà*.

A few years from now, as we say in Portuguese, "don't complain that I didn't warn you."

500 Days in Hell

Day 500
February 17

The number 500 brings with it a certain aura of magic.

Just this weekend, we had the 67th Edition of the Daytona 500 race, with the president's Beast parading on the International Speedway for two laps ahead of the pilots — for the "first time in history," I guess.

I can't imagine where we will be after 500 days of Trump's administration. It has not been 50 days yet, and the revelations are so stunning and so depressing that no honest, well-intentioned American can help being shocked, or so you would think.

Right?

Wrong. Just last week, while discussing a real-estate project on our mountain, a neighbor told me that he couldn't care less about the issue; what he truly couldn't accept was the "travesty in DC," with which I promptly and enthusiastically agreed.

However, to my utmost surprise, he later clarified that "the *Republican Congress* was more concerned about keeping their cushy jobs than doing their jobs of protecting and serving the nation" (emphasis added).

Excuse me?

It feels like we are standing in the midst of two dramatic flows of information that keep overflowing our brains, coming from the right and from the left. The expected result is confusion, a greater confusion than the one we had before — caused by the government's continuous lies and misinformation — and now caused by the excess of transparency and verified information.

Throughout my life, I had several periods in which I felt uneasy, frightened, not really knowing where the sensation was coming from. Until one day when, out of the blue, it was as if a curtain had been lifted and the situation fully exposed, generating a mixed feeling of relief, awareness... and uncertainty about what to do next.

That's how I'm feeling right now: relieved, and yet disgusted, utterly exhausted.

And it is with this mindset that, after an intense weekend of political discussions and senseless accusations and threats against Trump coming from our European friends in Munich, we arrive, today, at a most-feared milestone in the Israel-Gaza conflict: 500 days of intense war.

So far, despite Trump fulfilling his basic promise of total support for Israel and amidst contentious propositions, we are still being forced to accept the "dribs and drabs" presented by Hamas, with hostages being freed in homeopathic doses and in progressively worsening degrees of weariness and decrepitude.

The list of hostages still expected to be freed alive in Phase 1 of this torturous deal continues to include the Bibas family, on whom I have already given up.

Let's hope I'm wrong. Nothing would please me more at this point.

So, on this President's Day, don't forget the victims still kept captive, now for more than 500 days, by some of the cruelest criminals history has ever witnessed.

Have a nice week.

Never Forget

Day 504
February 21

Today, even *The Times of Israel* opted to hide the hideous Hamas billboard depicting Netanyahu as a vampire drinking the slaughtered Bibas's blood — in three languages, to make their message very clear — but its hideousness will not stop us.

Netanyahu didn't kill these hostages. Hamas did. They are the vampires, really, except that they seem to prefer cold blood.

I always avoided calling any modern public figure "Hitler," but finally, here you have it: Hamas is Nazism, on steroids.

We are lucky that they don't have the means and the organized minds typical of Germans, or we would never be able to sleep again (not that we are able to sleep now).

Below, you can see the whole picture.

Shabbat Shalom.

53 Years of Atrocities

March 15

Last night I watched the chilling and moving *September 5*, a recounting of the massacre of Israeli athletes in Munich from the interesting perspective of the ABC local studio during the 1972 Olympics.

It was the first broadcast live of a Palestinian terrorist attack perpetrated by an organization called Black September.

It wouldn't be the last.

It was a black September indeed. It was preceded by a black May, and would be followed by a black July, a black August, a black November, and, more recently, a black October.

I'm sure that, if I researched more, these monsters would fill out the whole calendar — since the creation of Israel in 1948. Taking this into account, we have not only 53, but 77 years of atrocities.

What are we going to do with these people?

October 7 Is Still Deadly Alive

Day 552
April 10

It's not that I forgot about October 7 — I will never forget — but we have had so many distractions lately here in the US that the tragedy and the pain went kind of to the back of my head for a while.

We had the recent elections, and the anticipation, and the inauguration. Then we had the executive orders, one after the other (they still keep coming every day, nonstop, as there's so much to fix in this country), the "resistance," the Wall Street roller coaster, and the tariffs dance, or stance.

It's all too much, I think you can understand. But on Tuesday night, when I saw the family of ex-hostages with their yellow scarves find their way to the podium in the Republicans' dinner, to join Donald Trump and thank him once again, everything came back at once.

There are still hostages in Gaza, and some of them are not dead.

The war is still raging.

October 7 is still deadly, and painfully alive — very much alive.

Last night, I dedicated some time to watch a remembrance interview with Douglas Murray, who is currently launching his book about what happened and what he witnessed firsthand in Gaza, *On Democracies and Death Cults: Israel and the Future of Civilization.*

This occasion is as good as ever to question the future of civilization. It's also a good week to reflect on freedom, slavery, faith, and endurance, given the theme of Passover: a celebration of 40 years in the desert after the escape from Egypt, with all the plagues involved.

Therefore, I ask myself a valid question, the same question probably asked by Moses when he saw the Promised Land from afar, knowing he would never get there alive: Is there hope?

On the other hand, a troubling doubt comes to mind: "Are the gifts of God enough?"

There are right teachings and wrong teachings, as we all know, and the question above reminds me of my aunt, who used to repeat it on the night of the Seder as an explanation for the song "Dayenu" — "enough" in Hebrew.

With all that has happened in the last few years, we are indeed tempted to say that "we have had enough," but the theme of the Passover song, of course, is the exact opposite: a list of blessings that God sent our way, and even if each one was the only one — according to the lyrics — it would have been enough.

I hope our future brings us the same certainty as the Seder night, faith and all.

Chag Sameach.

Another Hostage Has Been Freed

Day 584
May 12

It may seem like we forgot about Israel, but we have not.

It is a sad state of affairs, but it is true that, after a while, even the worst things we are facing start sounding as if there is "nothing new."

However, the outrage is the same, the pain is the same.

I was about to recommend that you watch an updated podcast about the war in Gaza when the news broke that Edan Alexander, the last American held hostage by these monsters, has been freed by Hamas.

Some reader on *The Free Press* complained that the Trump administration was freeing the American and leaving behind all the other 23, 20, 19, and dwindling...

Make no mistake: This is not Trump's fault. It's the fault of those emissaries of evil.

Pope Leo XIV has just said that "evil will not prevail."

We sincerely hope not.

Meanwhile, we remain hopeful that Trump's trip to the Middle East today will bear some fruit.

Quoting Douglas Murray, "Hamas must lose the war, and know it."

A Charismatic, Well-Meaning Idiot

Day 606
June 3

Greta Thunberg is an idiot. I mean, an official idiot, sorry, as she allegedly suffers from some self-described condition that actually turned her into much more than a simple idiot a few years ago, when she was in high school: It made her a hero.

Well done, Greta.

She was transformed into a symbol in the "struggle" against "climate change," and was suddenly seen everywhere with her tearful tone, even at the now-irrelevant United Nations.

She wanted to save the world.

Did she? Apparently, her activism has evolved: Her mortal enemies are now the Jews and the State of Israel. She even affirms, with utmost certainty, that the IDF attacked the little boat in which she's now braving the oceans in support of "Free Palestine."

She is charismatic.

She is (probably) well-meaning.

She is effective.

And still, she's an idiot, an absolutely useless idiot with no real information, just performative bravado and easy slogans.

It is obvious that she doesn't have a clue about the war she's waging, and yet, the real idiot is me, for giving her premium space in my little screen world.

Yes. The idiots are all of us.

A Jewish American Couple

Day 608
June 5

The fact that I hesitated for a few minutes between tagging this entry as "Israel at War" or "Quicknotes" — which would immediately relegate it to the bottom third of the page on my Substack — says something about this bloody war, and about all bloody wars, for that matter.

To be human is to be able to suffer a blow and still be capable of keeping your head up and moving on, or there wouldn't be anybody left in this world: left to mourn the dead, left to plan and execute vengeance, and, last but not least, left not to merely survive, but to keep having a life.

Yet, the pain remains. For each hostage released, for each body recovered, there is a tear to be shed — several tears, actually.

So today is the day of the charming couple whose bodies the IDF recovered from Gaza this Thursday morning.

I learned one or two things about them: They liked to take long walks, and it was during their morning walk, in their beloved kibbutz Nir Oz, that they were kidnapped and murdered — not necessarily in this order.

I'll quote *The Jerusalem Post*: "Judy was 70 years old, a mother of four, and a grandmother of seven. She was an English teacher specializing in children with special needs, and she worked with children with anxiety by using meditation and mindfulness methods."

She was a poet and entrepreneur and was dedicated to working for peace and brotherhood.

She had a habit of writing a haiku every morning and posting it on Facebook.

Gadi was "a gifted man, with sharp intellect and a love for wind instruments, which he played since he was a young child. He was a talented chef, and alongside his wife, Judy, he lived a healthy, active lifestyle."

All this was gone in a minute.

Life is short and unpredictable, so we should enjoy every minute as if it were the last. For some people, a regular minute of a regular day in the park can indeed be their last.

Someone already said that Israel will not leave anyone behind, alive or dead, so their bodies are now finally home.

Z"L Gadi Haggai and Judith Weinstein.

The Center of Evil

Day 618
June 15

Don't let yourselves be fooled by empty words: If Ali Khamenei is something "supreme," this would be "Supreme Evil."

I was engaged recently in a discussion about Muslims' reactions to Israel's actions in Iran.

"People are afraid of the United States," I've heard. "And they are being subjected to a heavy propaganda campaign" — no doubt hearing that the US is "Big Satan."

While the idea of "Satan" might be an illusion, evil certainly is not, so I answered: "Iran is not Islam. Iran today is evil, waging war against its own people," and I could have added, "And so is their alleged supreme leader," but I didn't.

I don't want to be perceived as anti-Islam. I'm frankly deadly tired of all that, and I wish for peace, but some things are obviously in the way.

I hope Israel got a substantial compensation for acquiescing to Trump's request not to "eliminate" Khamenei, I mean, if they acquiesced at all.

Maybe all this is no more than empty words. Or is it all theater, some kind of "masterful play" on the world stage to achieve a common goal?

Either way, we will know very soon.

If there is a God, regardless of what His name might be, I hope His justice prevails.

Have a nice week.

Finally, the New Hitler

June 19

It's official: According to *The Times of Israel* a few minutes ago, at the missile impact site — a major hospital in Be'er Sheva — the Minister of Defense, Israel Katz, declared that "Supreme Leader Ali Khamenei is the modern Hitler, and cannot continue to exist."

After progressives' overuse of the term totally erased the potential gravitas of comparing anybody to Hitler, we finally have a legitimate candidate for the role.

The *Free Presser* Bari Weiss is on TV advocating against Iran.

She's not alone.

Bari was supposed to be on vacation in Israel now, but given the latest attacks directed at densely populated areas, with an apparent shortage of interceptors from the famous Iron Dome, she had probably cancelled her dream trip.

Bari herself, the ultimate anti-Trumper, is now placing the hard decision in Trump's hands.

Everybody is.

All we can do is pray.

The Two Most Agonizing Weeks in Recent History

June 21

If I were a nail-biter, I wouldn't have any nails left by the 4th of July: This is the timeframe Trump gave us to make his decision on whether to give military support to Israel against its Uber-Enemy Iran.

By now, every single person in the US has turned into a specialist in nuclear fuel enrichment facilities, particularly those that are deeply buried within a mountain, like Fordo.

Just a few days ago, I didn't even know that something like that existed, and I would have preferred that it remained so. But we obviously don't hold the cards over the dire destiny that threatens us all, Little Satan and Big Satan included. (Oops, I just heard on TV the term "existential threat," and that's much more than a coincidence. It's sheer ubiquity these days.)

This morning I read a wonderful article in *The Free Press,* by Polina Fradkin, describing life in an Israeli bomb shelter that happens to be her bedroom. Again, such a pleasure, but I would much prefer never having to read it.

And yet.

Israel — and, by extension, all of us Jews — is finally facing its Armageddon, a violent battle with the other face of the good and evil coin, something I also didn't know existed.

Good and evil can be no more than morality plays, but these days, unfortunately, they have turned out to be the two faces of reality as well.

In a way, it's a relief. Our malevolent dance with Iran has lasted too long, hovering over our heads for more than 40 years and casting a shadow over Israeli society — Israel being described by Fradkin as "the strongest country in the world spiritually," and I add, but also militarily and in terms of intelligence, technology, and creativity, not to mention that the country also carries the dubiously honorific badge of being "the only democracy in the Middle East."

And yet, Israel's many enemies around the world — and counting — don't see that at all. They are not privy to the positive features that make Israel not only unique, but also, in the wise words of Melanie Phillips, "capable of elevating itself to the position of the next leader of the free world."

Right now, we don't know exactly what will happen, or when. Rumor has it that Trump's proverbial two weeks are both a platitude and an overused cliché, a theoretical deadline that the president "enjoys mentioning."

According to sources, the much-anticipated support in the form of B-2s — the only plane in the world capable of carrying the only bomb in the world capable of destroying the deeply-buried Fordo facility in Iran — can happen at any moment.

As I write, the B-2s are en route to the US military base in Guam.

I'm trying my best not to be bothered by Iran's bravado, threatening to destroy this and that. It is publicly known that Iran at present is a weak nation, no matter how many replacements its probably senile supreme leader nominates from his also deeply buried bunker — only God and the Israeli intelligence know where.

May it become his automatic grave.

May God protect us.

Have a nice Sunday.

It's a Done Deal

July 3

No, apparently, we're not dreaming. I've just heard the Speaker of the House, Mike Johnson, include the fact that Israel agreed to a 60-day ceasefire in his "list of victories just in the last two weeks." *The Times of Israel* just published the same regarding Hamas.

Oseh shalom aleinu.

Amen.

My Letter to The Times of Israel

Day 644

July 11

Dear Reader,

It is that time of the year that every writer fears. I'm so tired and so conflicted about so many issues that I haven't been able to put all this into words for a few days now.

In my head I tried several tricks: blaming my husband, telling jokes, confessing I'm exhausted and worn out.

Nothing worked.

Then, this morning, I came across a disgusting "investigation" by *The New York Times* accusing Prime Minister Netanyahu of horrible things, including the claim that the experienced politician is prolonging our pain on purpose.

I felt sick, considered writing about it, and then my whole revolt was distilled into a letter to *The Times of Israel* that, disgustingly enough, chose to propagate the "news."

Check it out below.

"Good morning.

It is disgusting that this newspaper, my preferred source of news for several years, especially after October 7, chooses to propagate lies "investigated" by The New York Times, affirming that Netanyahu is prolonging the war to stay in power.

Have you no shame?

Do you believe Netanyahu is the new Pol Pot? Better still, the new Hitler?

Jews around the world are in enough trouble regarding their support for Israel. People want to kill us. They want to "Kill the IDF." There is no need for The Times of Israel to put fuel into this fire.

Sincerely wishing for better and more fruitful days,

Shabbat Shalom."

Surrender!

Day 658

July 25

I don't know what's happening.

Nobody knows.

However, the international media is fully engaged in its condemnation of Israel, which is supposedly starving civilians to death in Gaza.

Is it true?

I doubt it.

There might be some truth to it, but I can ASSURE you this is not on Israel. It is on Hamas.

Let's revisit the facts. On October 7, 2023, 658 days ago, hundreds of savage terrorists invaded Israel and slaughtered more than a thousand people with extreme cruelty, let me remind you, including rape, decapitations, cooking babies in the oven, shooting parents in front of their children. A lot of these victims were very young concertgoers gathered near Gaza for a celebration of peace; others were well-known good people who dedicated their lives to help Gazans.

Yes, you heard me: to help Gazans. But this did not help them.

As part of the cruelty feast, hundreds of people, including some who were already dead, were kidnapped and taken hostage.

Many of them are still captive in Gaza. An estimated 20 of them are still alive (along with several corpses; I can't stop thinking about how they manage to keep those for bargaining purposes. In the freezer, you think?).

Israel was attacked with unheard-of violence and with more than one goal: An obvious intent was to provoke a reaction that would, in time, allow the terrorist group to "win the propaganda war" internationally.

Their project was extremely successful, and it still is, as the war is still ongoing.

So, now, Hamas has reached a new milestone in its peculiar war intended to destroy Israel and the Jews until nothing is left; we could call it "The Hunger Battle," and they are succeeding. Once again.

Israel, on the other hand, is fighting for its survival — for our survival, I should say — but nobody cares. The almighty Emmanuel Macron is poised to recognize the "Palestinian state" on Monday, winning the coveted prize of being the "first Western nation" to do so.

What Palestinian state?

There is no Palestinian state, and Hamas made sure of it.

In the news today, we can read that "if Hamas doesn't want to make a ceasefire deal, its leaders will be 'hunted down,'" according to Trump.

What people don't understand, or don't want to understand, is that there is an easy, fast, effective way to finish the suffering on both sides.

After being largely defeated by the Israeli armed forces, the spectacular IDF, Hamas has only one path ahead: They *must* surrender.

Yes. With the miraculous waving of a beautiful white flag, we would get rid of all this "news" of starvation, genocide, and the like, overnight.

"There is no genocide in Gaza," I read this week in an excellent essay written by the "war scholar" John Spencer.

There might be hunger in Gaza to some degree, but this is a manufactured pain.[8]

---

[8] For those of you who would like to know more, I recommend that you watch this video, in which Chuck Holton, a former military specialist turned podcaster, visited the place from which food is distributed to Gazans, protected by the IDF.

Am I clear?
Release the hostages.
Surrender.
Shabbat Shalom.

Melanie and the BBC

Day 663
July 30

I have been wrong a lot lately, and on serious issues. The latest was my faux pas regarding "Sir" Keir Starmer, which I thought, precisely a year ago, was a "good man," mostly because he "loved classical music."

It turns out that Starmer is *not* a good man.

"He is monstrous," says Melanie Phillips.

My indignation knows no limits. So, this pompous moral midget is now demanding that Israel "accept a ceasefire"?

Let me be clear: Israel *already* accepted a ceasefire, and invariably, in each instance, Hamas refused to do so, so how is Israel supposed to save itself from probable elimination?

Israel had also accepted the two-state solution, and I mean, *repeatedly*, including in Oslo, Camp David and other occasions, involving several generations of Palestinian leaders over the years.

Until we stopped... after the country was savagely attacked 663 days ago. (The number of the beast, 666, is fast approaching, and the devil will come to collect his due.)

So, right now, the majority of Israel's reasonable citizens, who were once in favor of a Palestinian state, cannot, and will not even talk about it.

Yes, because Hamas's (real) conditions are *not* that Israel accepts a ceasefire, but that Israel *ceases to exist*.

There are many loud voices, much better than mine, making themselves heard right now. And especially because this new "element" on the diplomacy chessboard is coming from the UK, I beg you to check out Melanie Phillips, the knowledgeable British journalist who now lives in Israel — a country that, despite the raging war, she considers safer for a Jew than her native England, and the latest facts are proving her right.

Today, Melanie writes about the BBC, which is trashing its own reputation as "the world's most trusted and influential broadcaster" by publishing daily lies about the war in Gaza.

Melanie's work is essential these days, effective, disturbing — as it should be.

Don't listen to me.

Listen to her.

Because she knows.

David Grossman Drinks the Kool-Aid

Day 665

August 1

The Times of Israel, Friday, August 1, 665 days after Hamas committed a "classic" genocide against the Israeli people: "With 'broken heart,' author David Grossman calls Israeli actions in Gaza 'genocide'."

The literary giant is not the only one with a broken heart. My heart is broken, and the pieces are shattered in an unrecoverable manner when I see these so-called "moral giants," one after the other, fall into temptation like dominoes.

I feel sick.

I want to die.

I cry non-stop.

What's happening? Are these people now incapable of controlling their own impulse to give in to the propaganda mob?

What do they want?

Have they no hearts?

Do they not bleed?

Even the otherwise antisemitic-leaning readers of *The Times* of London understand the situation better: A vast majority of comments in today's edition opted for criticizing their failing Prime Minister, explaining with utmost clarity what the real situation in the field is — check it out for yourself.

One of them even came up with a brilliant parody: "Imagine President Roosevelt had a gun to Churchill's head and demanded that he feed the poor Nazis." Others reminded us that a siege is the most effective military strategy there is, although this is not what's happening.

And it's not that this growing approval of Hamas's criminal plan is going to help the Palestinians themselves either, as it is clear to almost everybody that there is no such thing as a Palestinian state. According to international law, "Palestine doesn't have the characteristics that a state needs to have. It doesn't have sovereignty. It doesn't really control its own borders. It's not able to behave as a state."

The only good thing that could come out of this mess is that, if they *did* have a state, the Palestinians would lose their "eternal refugees" status by living in their own sovereign state — which would translate into a permanent loss of billions of dollars in free money.

The curious thing is that people do recognize and understand that they are falling victim to a propaganda scam, like the dreadful, despicable, inhumane hoax involving a sick child — perpetrated through the skillful "elimination" of the healthy brother by the sick baby's side to reinforce the idea of starvation and genocide — later "corrected" by *The New York Times*.

On the other hand, the Arab nations, in fact, understand what the truth is, as you can see in a rare agreement against Hamas: "At a UN gathering on Tuesday, Arab and Muslim countries condemned the Hamas invasion and massacre in an unprecedented joint declaration and called on Hamas to lay down its arms and free all the hostages, as part of a call to end the war in Gaza and progress to a two-state solution to the Israeli-Palestinian conflict."

Really? Wouldn't that be awesome?

Now, when a "literary giant" like Grossman and other luminaries in Israel decide to join the lynching mob, all seems to be lost. It is literally the collective suicide of a national identity.

Shabbat Shalom.

Courtesy of Al-Qassam Brigade

Day 666
August 2

Hello, France.
Hello, UK.
Hello, Canada.

This video is brought to you as a courtesy of your new friends in the political arena.

Enjoy.

For those of you with the capacity to understand who this is — Evyatar David, a young Israeli being kept hostage for 666 days, and, yes, ***subjected to deliberate starvation*** by his Palestinian captors (a.k.a. Hamas) — I beg you to please help the Western world understand who they are dealing with as well.

Instead of giving them a country, demand that they end this modern-day Holocaust.

Because that's the right thing to do, not threatening Israel instead.

Jesus Was a Refugee

August 27

No. He wasn't.

The propaganda campaign in favor of illegal immigration is from the Biden years, but I only watched it a few minutes ago, and the story gets it all wrong.

The reason why Mary and Joseph had to escape, described in modern terms, is limited to only one word: antisemitism. And I mean, hatred of Jews.

Jesus, by the way, while being the core reason for that story, was not even part of it until just hours earlier, unless you consider a fetus in a mother's womb a human being — something that the "progressives" behind this "campaign" don't even believe in.

Speaking of which, a member of this "sanctified" group protected by these despicable people just went into a church at a Catholic school in Minneapolis, killed a 5-year-old and a 10-year-old, and injured 20 others.

Jesus, I'm sure, would never "get" that.

Who does?

Crazy people like the ones behind this despicable campaign I've just seen on TV, that was launched in 2023, which means it had been around for at least two years, brainwashing their way to power.

No pasarán.

***

A short, but necessary note: Google Gemini refused to review this article. I sometimes use Gemini to review my articles, and I pay it for doing it, but this one was considered "hate speech," I guess you know why.

What You Will NOT See in Today's News

September 7

You've probably noticed by now that I have been absent a lot from this most cherished space.

I can't explain it, except by telling you that, when I write something, it's because I receive a "higher" calling — whatever that means — an irresistible impulse to just stop everything else I'm doing and sit and write.

Like now, for example.

My friend and compatriot from Florida just sent me a link showing Brazilians demonstrating in London in favor of Israel.

I don't usually write about this kind of stuff, but today is Brazil's Independence Day and, as (maybe) you already know, Brazil has been taken over by, let's say, "forces of evil," which manifest in several ways, such as the endless persecution of former president Jair Bolsonaro and a clear, against-all-odds support for the "Palestinian cause."

Oswaldo Aranha must be turning in his grave.

For those of you who haven't heard of him, the Brazilian diplomat Oswaldo Aranha was the chair of the United Nations General Assembly session that approved the partition plan for Palestine, giving birth to the State of Israel in 1948.

Please make a mental note that the "Palestine" then has nothing to do with the "Palestine" now. It was merely a territorial designation used by the British Empire, which had taken it from the Ottoman Empire.

I'm surprised Lula's claws have been kept away from this page on the Brazilian government official website, describing the long-standing diplomatic relations between my first two countries of citizenship — the United States now being the third and the only one I officially recognize in the form of a passport.

Maybe this government's officials simply don't know how to read, one wonders! They wouldn't be outliers when it comes to radical leftists. As you might know, leftists' methods and grammar recently adopted in the United States have resulted in children's illiteracy.

So, back in London, the Brazilians were celebrating their Independence Day when they came across a pro-Israel demonstration criticizing the upcoming approval of a "Palestinian state" by the UK government, and the two crowds mingled together, celebrating the Jews and the State of Israel at the same time.

You could check this news on the private Instagram profile shared with me by my Floridian pal. Otherwise, don't bother looking it up on Google. I had to go to DuckDuckGo to find something in that regard, and even there, it wasn't much.

That's the world we're currently living in, my friends. The forces of good seem to be forced into oblivion, but hopefully not for long.

Happy Brazil's Independence Day y'all! (An oxymoron, I must add.)

Have a nice week, y'all!

May We All Be Inscribed in the Book of Life

September 29

There is not much to say about the joint conference with Trump and Netanyahu that has just resumed at the White House, except to highlight the perhaps not-so-obvious importance of its timing: two days before the next Yom Kippur, which will mark the second anniversary of the terrifying Hamas attack of October 7.

A few months after the attack, we could read on social media the bleak conclusion that, as a result of October 7, "on Simchat Torah we learned that there is no God. On Hanukkah we understood that there are no miracles."

It is in the human purview to find the capacity to forgive and forget.

We will never forget. But on the eve of this Yom Kippur, let's hope we can find within ourselves the capacity to forgive.

G'Mar Chatimah Tovah. May we all be inscribed in the Book of Life.

Hanoi Jane and the Nobel Prize

October 4

It might look like a distant, unachievable dream, but as I write, Jared Kushner and Steve Witkoff are heading to Cairo for "final talks to end the war in Gaza."

The timing couldn't have been more surreal: It was the first thing I heard as I emerged from a TGA episode, my fourth event from a rare condition — Transient Global Amnesia — which, according to the Mayo Clinic, rarely happens more than twice in a lifetime, "an episode of confusion that comes on suddenly in a person who is otherwise alert."

It's a frightening condition, I give you that, but otherwise totally harmless, not caused by neurological diseases such as epilepsy or stroke. More importantly, it has nothing to do with Alzheimer's, and it's probably due to excess stress or physical effort. At the time, I was at home alone, cutting a piece of wood flooring with a Japanese hand saw, believe it or not.

But enough with all this; I just wanted to add it as a setting detail, so you can understand how incredible it felt to "wake up" to the news that Hamas had, in principle, accepted Trump's conditions for peace: namely, the immediate return of all the hostages, dead or alive — who, according to the terrorist bunch made into heroes by the left, are "Israeli prisoners."

All I could manage to do was start to cry.

Let me be clear: These are not prisoners, but the unfortunate victims of the most horrible, most violent, most gruesome attack on Jews since the Holocaust. And yet, the perpetrators were made into "heroes" by the do-gooders of this world, suddenly afflicted by some kind of hypnotic delusion that prevents them from seeing reality.

The latest, loosely associated consequence of this global madness was the attack on the synagogue in Manchester, England, during Yom Kippur prayers, leaving two dead and several wounded. If you want to know more or understand better what's happening in England right now, I recommend that you read Matt Goodwin's Substack.

We can only hope that this "dark period" in our lives — which includes Covid and Biden's "séjour" in the White House — goes away together with Hamas, which, despite their initial "disagreement," will not be allowed to be part of the "new" Gaza Strip —

not by Israel, not by Trump, and not by the Arab countries that Jared and Steve have managed to put together around this deal.

Hamas has lost the war. Period.

The second thing that came to my mind was that, if Biden hadn't been president, the war in Gaza would never have happened, and that thought made me cry even more. But it's too late for that now: Trump *is* president, and, in another promise fulfilled, the war in Gaza will end — which should, and hopefully will, earn him the Nobel Peace Prize.

Even Hillary Clinton seems to agree. However, that's not where Jane Fonda and her leftist peers are heading, and definitely not what the stunningly beautiful almost 90-year-old actress means by "dark times." What she means is that Trump is a dictator, a tyrant, and a fascist who has destroyed the First Amendment and other freedoms in the United States…

Shame!

How can these people live with themselves? Don't they have enough blood on their hands already? Can't they see where their misguided perceptions are leading them? And potentially all of us?

We can only hope, and hope is, indeed, the dominant tone in the aftermath of this Yom Kippur.

May this war never reach its dreadful second anniversary, which happens in just three days.

May we be capable of believing in miracles again.

Have a nice weekend.

Greta Thunberg Was Never Brilliant

October 8

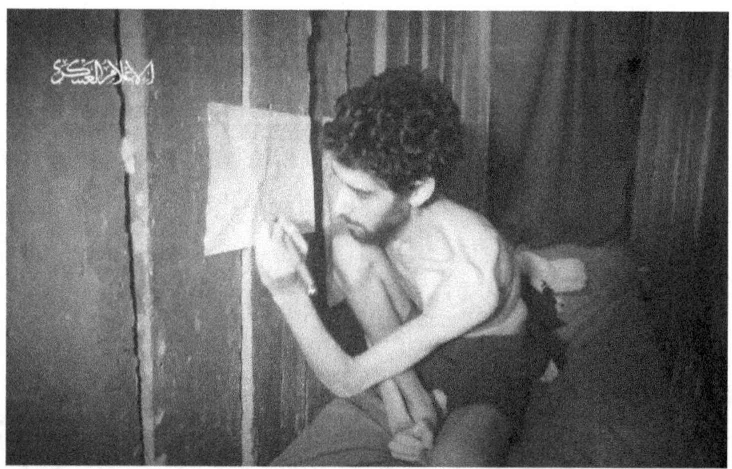

Israeli hostage Evyatar David starving in a tunnel in Gaza, depicted by Greta
Thunberg as a "Palestinian" prisoner.

As the old saying goes, "A man who stands for nothing will fall
for anything," but that's not exactly the case for the eternal child
activist from Sweden, Greta Thunberg.

Greta Thunberg is not an Ikea of intelligence, so to speak, and
she also has a penchant for the wrong causes. In other words,
she stands for anything that "sounds" like something worth
fighting for, but, in fact, is not.

What kind of unexplained power does this woman have?

I fail to grasp it.

Her militance against "climate change" gave new meaning to
what President Trump now calls "the con job of the century" —
or at least of two centuries — which basically gave birth to the
DEI craze and all the lunacy that took over our lives gradually, and
then suddenly, during the Covid years. This is exactly the same
craziness we are being forced to battle against right now, with a

huge emphasis on the upside-down and inside-out beliefs of the Gretas Thunbergs of this world, who seem to have multiplied like maggots after October 7.

The insanity reached a malevolent kind of peak when, yesterday, while being deported from Israel after another "flotilla flop," the great Greta published a photo of a "Palestinian prisoner being mistreated by Israel."

According to the *New York Post*, "'The suffering of Palestinian prisoners is not a matter of opinion — it is a fact of cruelty and dehumanization. Humanity cannot be selective. Justice cannot have borders,' read Greta's post, made in collaboration with a slew of other activists." Except that... it was, in fact, a picture of the Israeli hostage Evyatar David, being starved to death in a tunnel in Gaza for more than two years.

A touch of especially bad taste is that, right now, there are negotiations being held in Sharm El-Sheikh, Egypt, to return the hostages and end the war — being regarded by all as the best chance for peace the region has ever had.

According to the families of these last hostages, in a letter to the Norwegian Nobel Committee, "[the] US president 'brought us light in our darkest times' with his efforts to secure the hostages' release."

My hopes are high — for the end of the war, of course; for a Nobel Peace Prize for Trump, they are close to zero.

It is true that for some voices, traditionally closer to the left, the truth seems to be sinking in, as you could see this week in an interesting conversation between Sam Harris and Dan Senor. The podcast, recorded last Friday, has two high points: first, Harris highlights how the staunchest defenders of Palestinians didn't say a word about the chances of Trump's 21-point plan, now 100% in Hamas's court; and second, Harris read, live on the air, that Hamas had just accepted the plan — so to speak.

Of course, when it comes to Hamas, things will never be easy. They already started with demands that Israel return all prisoners arrested for participating in and organizing the October 7 attack.

Should Israel do it?

I don't know. The return of the hostages is an absolute priority. However, it was exactly what happened when 1,000 dangerous criminals — among them the late Yahya Sinwar, whose life was saved in prison by an Israeli doctor — were exchanged for a single soldier, Gilad Shalit, in 2011.

The rest is history. If it were not for Shalit, maybe October 7 would never have happened. Who knows?

Ask Greta!

It's Over (Live from Tel-Aviv's Hostages Square)

October 8

"I am very proud to announce that Israel and Hamas have both signed off on the first Phase of our Peace Plan. This means that ALL of the Hostages will be released very soon, and Israel will withdraw their Troops to an agreed upon line as the first steps toward a Strong, Durable, and Everlasting Peace. All Parties will be treated fairly! This is a GREAT Day for the Arab and Muslim World, Israel, all surrounding Nations, and the United States of America, and we thank the mediators from Qatar, Egypt, and Turkey, who worked with us to make this Historic and Unprecedented Event happen. BLESSED ARE THE PEACEMAKERS!

DONALD J. TRUMP

PRESIDENT OF THE UNITED STATES OF AMERICA"

The 100-Year War Is Over

October 13

"Todah, Elohim, todah!" — "Thank You, God, thank You!" says the father, greeting the son he hasn't seen or heard from for exactly two years today, according to the Hebrew calendar.

It's Simchat Torah once again, the Jewish holiday that celebrates the completion of the yearly reading of the Torah, 12 days after Yom Kippur, when we ask God to inscribe us in the Book of Life.

One wonders: Is there really a God to listen?

For Guy Gilboa — the young man in the video I was watching — and the other 19 Israeli men released from captivity today, and their families, the answer is yes: Their prayer has been answered.

I ask your permission to erase the harsh words I said two years ago, when I affirmed that God didn't exist. I also said, during Hanukkah of that same year, that there were no miracles.

I was wrong.

There is a God. And miracles do happen.

"Miracle," of course, is the name being given to the steady actions of President Trump and his brilliant team of negotiators, Koffy & Kushner — though I'm sure several other elements were involved.

Boldness.

Intelligence.

Persistence.

Faith.

During my lifetime, I have witnessed many wars in the Middle East, each one charged with different emotions — pride, pain, possibilities. I once believed this series had begun in 1947, with the War of Independence, but I was wrong.

Only a couple of days ago, when I watched the timely new movie *Shoshana*, I understood that this war actually started around 1925, with the actions of the first Israeli heroes against the British in pursuit of the right to a homeland; so, on and off, we have been at war in the Middle East for a hundred years.

My whole lifetime and beyond!

Starting today, God willing, there will be an empty hole in my life, the space previously occupied by concerns about Israel and the region — felt more intensely than ever over the past two years.

May this hole be filled, forever, with hope and joy.

Thank you, President Trump.

Blessed are You, Adonai our God, Sovereign of all, who has kept us alive, sustained us, and brought us to this day.

Picture of the Day, Sharm El-Sheikh

October 1

Arab and world leaders sign the Peace Treaty, a.k.a. the Gaza Peace Plan, with Trump at the center of the table.

Wow.

Trump's Brilliant Strategy

October 14

You heard it here first: This morning, while working out, I had an epiphany and suddenly understood what Trump is up to.

Did you notice that throughout this long day (it started around 2 a.m. EST), including those typical marathon speeches by our president — both in Jerusalem and in Sharm El-Sheikh — in front of millions of viewers, Trump did not mention a "Palestinian state" once?

"Sir" Keir was visibly upset as Trump accepted the Medal of the Nile (read that fast). Macron and the UN's Guterres were nowhere to be seen. Even the court's favorite, Giorgia Meloni, was obliterated by a front row of, so to speak, arch-billionaire sheikhs.

Abbas was mentioned *en passant*, apparently watching "from the gods." I confess I didn't see him, nor did I miss him one little bit.

Trump talked and talked and talked, and, like a legitimate real-estate mogul, described how his co-signatories had a huge amount of money ready to invest in the "reconstruction project."

Not a word about the "mandatory" Palestinian state — without which, according to the three Western stooges, peace in the region would never be achieved. Not a word.

Bear with me for a moment: Trump's strategy clearly included the radical reduction, or explicit obliteration, of a partner named "Hamas," or even of an entity called "the Palestinian people." With luck, the new, beautiful Gaza will become a sophisticated resort — a charming, wealthy section of its neighbor Egypt, not by coincidence the host of the Peace Summit.

Hamas will be fortunate to survive at the stables.

Now, imagine a group of rich investors who get together for a real-estate project. Who do you think the property rights will belong to?

By obliterating even the mention of Hamas and distributing the shares of his next development among his Summit peers, Trump sealed the destiny of his opponent more effectively than with a nuclear bomb.

That's what I call "investment savvy."

It seems incredible that the solution to this puzzling problem was so in our faces, and nobody had figured it out until now.

Well, sort of. Several years ago, during Trump's first term, Jared Kushner and a dream team of young geniuses had this epiphany first with the Abraham Accords, unfortunately stopped in their tracks by Covid and the unfortunate election of Joe "Autopen" Biden.

But that's all in the past now.

Mark my words: It won't take long for Gaza to be elected as the world's #1 honeymoon destination.

Maktub.

Part Four

Afterthoughts

Art, Intellect, Excellence. Who Cares?

November 7

Remind me: When was the last time the Palestinian Philharmonic Orchestra performed in Paris? What's the name, I forgot, of that famous, wonderful Palestinian violinist? How many Palestinians have won a Nobel Prize in science? Or found a revolutionary treatment for an incurable disease? Or created incredible software?

Right.

NEVER.

NONE.

IT NEVER HAPPENED.

IT'S UNHEARD OF.

I understand. You don't like classical music. You don't appreciate science. You despise technology.

Alright.

When was the last time a Palestinian singer won the Eurovision?

No?

Let's try the other way around: When was the last time a group of masked young Israelis invaded a music festival, killed and kidnapped more than 500 innocent young people? Raped the women? Took people hostage, dead or alive — yes, they even took cadavers hostage — to "negotiate" them later? Decapitated babies, or cooked them in the oven? And proudly recorded everything on their cell phones to show their parents?

Right.

NEVER.

So why is the world cheering these savages? Again and again?

Honestly. Why are brilliant young people in New York signing up for Sharia law?

Oh, yes. They are not very brilliant, perhaps?

I'm sorry if I sound angry.

No. I'm not... sorry.

Honestly, I'm tired of this nonsense, of this constant attack on civilization, of these inverted values, day in and day out. I can't stand another minute of this shit.

If you go back through history, you won't find a single reason why these people, especially young people, hate Jews so much. Historically, Jews never tried to erase Muslims or anybody else. Mostly, they were the ones being erased.

Could it be envy? I wonder.

Now, in principle, I'm for freedom, for everyone to live their lives as they see fit. But not when they are destroying mine, without a second thought.

This might be the problem with modern democracies: They don't respect themselves, they don't praise or prioritize their own values, and, ultimately, that's why they are about to lose them.

These people "protesting" are so ignorant, so stupid, it hurts.

Why, remind me, are we allowing this? In the name of what? Remind me?

I honestly thought that, once we reached an agreement in Gaza, this nonsense would stop, but it doesn't seem like it's going to. Young people today are deluded, vulnerable to racist tropes, yes, what can be more racist than antisemitism? Remind me?

And to wrap it up: Why, remind me, is America powerful?

Ok, I get it: the founders, the Constitution, the freedom of speech, and so on, but let's face it, America today is powerful because it defended the Jews and defeated evil incarnate in the Third Reich, the infamous Adolf Hitler, so popular among these dissenters who, today, think America itself is the Third Reich (and that you know who is Hitler).

Does that make any sense?

Just think about it. Dedicate five or ten precious minutes of your wasted lives to reflect on the meaning of all this, and that is... NONE.

This must stop. Somebody with power must find a way, and they will.

Until then... Let's hope and pray.

Shabbat Shalom.

It's Not Over Until It's Over

Day 815

December 29

As I wrap up this historical saga, I wonder if the title of this book is, in fact, a dreadful prophecy nobody wants to fulfill.

Will the war truly last until Day 1000?

I hope not.

The new year is around the corner, for the third time. Not long ago, Trump was holding a joint press conference with Ne-

tanyahu in Mar-a-Lago, the nth one since all this has started —
yes, I lost count.

Among other things, Netanyahu granted Trump a special
prize that had never been given to a non-Israeli, honoring him as
the best friend Israel has ever had in the White House.

And yet, peace remains elusive.

We're on the brink of "Phase Two," but Phase One was never
completed.

I was surprised to see that, today, Netanyahu still wore the
tragic yellow pin on his lapel, so I decided to do some research,
et voilà, I discovered, with astonishment, that there is still one
remaining hostage to be returned.

True: Staff Sgt. Maj. Ran Gvili is not technically a hostage. He
is a corpse.

And yet, "Israeli officials say the failure to return Gvili's remains has directly contributed to the current deadlock in ceasefire discussions. One security source warned that the impasse
carries immediate consequences for Hamas. 'We are apply-
ing very strong and clear pressure. Until Gvili's remains are returned, there will be no progress. Everyone knows we are in an
interim situation,'" according to sources.

It is not the only hurdle negotiators are facing. "Phase Two"
includes the most difficult achievements of all so far: Hamas
must disarm and return all its weapons.

Will they do it?

We don't know.

The media no longer dedicates hours of its coverage to the
"war in Gaza." Sparse and rare newscasts now show occasional
efforts by Palestinians to rebuild their lives. However, *The Times
of Israel*, which became my go-to news source throughout these
long three years that rushed by like a bad dream, keeps counting

the days, something I had neglected in these least few entries — so today is Day 815.

One hundred eighty-five to go.

I find some comfort in putting numbers on things, as a reminder of my days as a "numerologist," or perhaps, more enlighteningly, an influence from Rashi, the famous medieval scholar who interpreted the Biblical message by attributing numerical values to each Hebrew letter in the text.

May my prediction fail.

May peace be with us, with all of us.

Post-Scriptum

The Last Hostage Has Returned Home

Day 843
January 26, 2026

Police officer Master Sgt. Ran Gvili

The last hostage has been returned to Israel.
The nightmare is finally over. After 843 days, 12 hours, and 6 minutes, the Hostages Square clock went dark in Tel Aviv.

On this historic day, *The Times of Israel* also stopped counting.

What a relief.

Ran Gvili's body was found in a cemetery in Gaza. According to *The Times of Israel*, "250 bodies were checked and returned to their graves" before Gvili's remains were identified through dental and fingerprint matching.

Z"L.

Never again.

Noga Sklar is a writer, publisher, and professional translator. Born in Tiberias, Israel, she lived for many years in Rio de Janeiro, a city she later left to take refuge with her husband Alan in a mountain paradise, amid the Atlantic Forest.

Her encounter with Alan gave new impetus to her life and literary career. Based on their online interactions, Noga wrote her best-selling novel *No Degrees of Separation* — a passionate diary described by the writer and psychoanalyst Ana Cecilia Carvalho as a modern *Song of Songs*.

An American citizen since 2016, Noga lives in Greenville, South Carolina, where she works as a technical and literary trans-lator and offers consultancy to authors seeking to expand their market. She continues to write and publish her essays in a unique voice, which can be found on her Substack, *The Middle Way*.

Printed in the USA
Greenville, SC
April 21 2026

www.ingramcontent.com/pod-product-compliance
Lightning Source LLC
Chambersburg PA
CBHW071208240726
48654CB00009B/691